Interpretive Undercurrents

MRCA

Interpretive Undercurrents

by Carl A. Strang, Ph.D.

Drawings by Scott Patton

Cover design by Alea Hashimoto

THE NATIONAL ASSOCIATION FOR INTERPRETATION

Portions of this book appeared earlier in periodicals published by the National Association for Interpretation and one of its predecessors, the Association of Interpretive Naturalists, and are reproduced with permission here. Those periodicals include *Legacy*, the *Buffalo Bull*, and the original *Journal of Interpretation*.

Acknowledgements

This book would not have appeared without the support of NAI members (and, earlier, AIN members), especially those of Region 5, over the past 15 years. In particular I want to mention the editor of the *Legacy*, Alan Leftridge, and past and present editors of the *Buffalo Bull* who have worked with me: Cem Basman, Dale Goodner, Steve Aultz and Jean Knight, Dave Brooks and Mary Rice. Brook McDonald deserves the credit for approaching me with the idea for this book in the spring of 1998. The Iowa Association of Naturalists secured the Scott Patton drawings and made them available. The Board for Region 5 enthusiastically encouraged this project and paid for it. I am grateful to Nancy Nichols of the National Office for helping with administrative details.

The Regional Board encouraged me to put this book together without an editor or, rather, to edit it myself. I realize that this is not the recommended procedure. On the one hand, most of this book already has appeared in NAI publications and thus was exposed to editorial scrutiny. On the other hand, it's not simply a compilation. I rewrote parts of it so as to flow together better, and I expanded some topics with new material. Thus, despite the presence of NAI's logo on this book, the responsibility for its text is mine.

I am proud to be part of the Forest Preserve District of DuPage County and its Willowbrook Wildlife Center. I am especially indebted to Willowbrook's Curator, Marcy Rogge, for the free rein she has given me in creating Willowbrook's educational offerings. Without such a testing ground, this book would have no validity.

I dedicate this book to all my teachers, first of all my parents, Ted and Chuckie Strang.

Table of Contents

Introduction

I was 7 or 8 years old, and I sat on the shore of Hawk Lake, near my home town of Culver, in northern Indiana. Beside me was my older friend, on summer break from his undergraduate studies. He pointed to several great blue herons feeding at the far side of the lake, where the oak woodland lining the shore formed a dark backdrop against which the tall, pale birds contrasted. As various other birds flew past us, he spoke of how different kinds of birds could be distinguished in flight. I remember questioning him eagerly, but I also remember the peaceful grace of the herons, the beauty of that warm evening.

A year or two later, a Culver Military Academy faculty member took his son and me for a mid-winter forest walk at the Bird Sanctuary, a morainal beech-maple forest on Academy property. I was enchanted by all the little wonders and signs of life. In the dusk a barred owl called, then flew, just visible among the distant trees. We had found some owl pellets. As he drove me home, the teacher explained that experts could identify the species of owl which had cast a pellet. Who were these people, these experts? I wished I could do things like that.

Both of these men were interpreters, though they probably never had heard of the art. Both strongly influenced my path, my career choices, my orientation toward the world. A profound part of those memories was the setting. I recall especially the excitement I felt, balanced or perhaps augmented by the beauty of the scenes.

Apart from their lasting impact on my life, these experiences illustrate some important aspects of interpretation. It wasn't just the interpreters: the setting was very important, and I was a full partner in the process as well. Emotionally and spiritually I was touched deeply by these experiences. Remove any of these elements: land-scape, interpreter or me, and there would have been no strong memories to relate, no story to tell.

I believe that much of what is critical to the interpretive process is subtle and inadequately addressed by the interpretive literature. This book is about some of those subtleties. I call them interpretive undercurrents, and their study is Deep Interpretation. The most significant interpretive undercurrents are the ones that result in profound, life-changing moments like the ones from my life I just described. If I ever comprehend such interpretive moments so well that I can consciously control and shape them, it will be time for Volume Two. Until then...

After much searching for an appropriate symbol or metaphor, I have come to regard interpretation as a process composed of three overlapping circles (*Fig. 1*). The circle of the community represents the resource being interpreted and, in some cases, the Earth as a whole. We are a part of that community. The circle of the interpreter, and the circle of the individual for whom or with whom the interpretation is taking place complete the picture. By understanding our communities thoroughly, understanding people and focusing on them individually, polishing our interpretive technique, growing in love within each of the three circles, and then following our intuition, we give those interpretive moments their best opportunity to emerge.

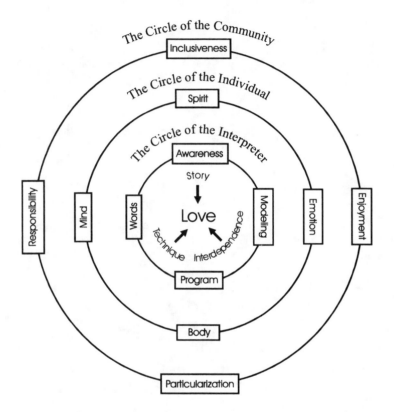

Figure 1:Pictorial form of the Interpretive Undercurrents model.

Part 1: The Circle of the Community

Part 1: The Circle of the Community

Introduction

It is through community that we live most of our lives, and it is through community that environmental and social problems both arise and are solved. My meaning of "community" here is unconventional. *Webster's Third New International Dictionary* defines community as "a body of individuals organized into a unit or manifesting usually with awareness some unifying trait." Ecologists also use the word to describe the organisms living together in an area, i.e., an ecological community is the living component (as opposed to physical properties and processes) of an ecosystem. I believe that ecological communities and human social communities are not separate in any significant sense. We are embedded in our landscape. We depend upon it for our survival. It impacts us, and we certainly have an impact on it.

Thus the community concept is ripe for interpreters to use in bringing together environmental and social concerns, showing people that there is a common denominator to our problems and opening the door to a common solution. Both sets of problems are complex, both stem from the fundamental principles and structure of our society, and neither can be solved without the other being healed, as well. Thus, interpreters whose work touches on environmental problems, or whose constituents are impacted in some way by social problems (and who is not?) can add power and completeness to their efforts by taking an inclusive view of environmental and social concerns. When we ignore some of these problems, we can be taken as irrelevant or uncaring by those who are impacted by them. We should be able to answer strongly the impoverished inner city resident, struggling family farmer, or drug

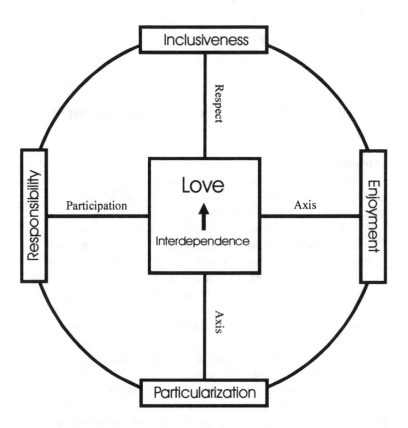

Figure 2: The Circle of the Community

addict who questions the relevance of environmental concerns to their lives. At the same time our holistic view of things should enable us to offer a bridge for environmentalists who fail to see a connection between their issues and human social problems. Most important, we need to reach children, demonstrating to them the connectedness of all the aspects of our lives.

I am a naturalist at the Willowbrook Wildlife Center, a facility of the Forest Preserve District of DuPage County, Illinois. Much of Willowbrook's work has to do with mediating in various ways the interactions between our human constituents and their wild animal neighbors. Some of these interactions are mutually beneficial, as when people landscape their yards with wildlife in mind. Other interactions are antagonistic, for instance when a homeowner and a mother squirrel compete for the use of an attic. Still others are more complex.

Drop-Kick was an exhibit raccoon at the Willowbrook Wildlife Center for a few years. He had been taken from the wild as an infant and raised as a pet. The man who had raised him lost interest, and gave or sold the young raccoon to a next-door neighbor. When the raccoon reached the point in its development where it normally would leave its mother and establish itself elsewhere, and that instinct was frustrated by captivity, he began to growl, snarl and bite. The neighbor put the raccoon in a bag and viciously drop-kicked it over the fence, back to the man who originally had taken the animal from the wild. He took it to Willowbrook with a fractured pelvis and other injuries from which the raccoon was unable to recover sufficiently for release, and so he became an exhibit animal. Drop-Kick would not have been able to live well in the wild in any case: his opportunity for proper social development with other raccoons had been taken from him. This story reveals the complexity of human relations with one anther and with wild things.

When tourists visit an interpretive site, they breathe the oxygen, drink the water, and occupy space in the landscape. Their footsteps and presence influence the lives of plants and animals there. The landscape in turn has an impact on the visitors. It inhabits their memories and influences their behavior. Visitors inhale oxygen emitted by local plants, which in turn absorb carbon dioxide the visitors exhale. In this way a part of each visitor's body remains behind, becoming plant tissue, and that carbon is passed on to herbivores and decomposers, predators and parasites, long after the tourist departs. Thus the resource being interpreted, the visitor, and the interpreter, all are part and parcel of the same community.

Components of Community

After thinking about it, I have concluded that at least five conceptual elements are needed to form a dynamic, healthy community (*Fig. 2*). Each is essential, and collectively they are sufficient, in my opinion, to define "community." The five components are interdependence, particularization, inclusiveness, responsibility, and enjoyment.

Interdependence is central to the community concept. The fact that living beings have needs which must be met by other living beings is the essential foundation upon which any community is based. Our needs as animals include basic survival requirements such as food, water, and oxygen; we need a healthy Earth to provide these things. Humans also have a variety of social needs. Safety, belonging, and esteem are examples of needs which we depend on others to fulfill at least in part. These "others" are the members of both our human community and our ecological community.

If we were not dependent upon one another, and upon the landscape, there would be no need for community to exist in the first place. But I also believe that interdependence does not occupy the center of the community circle by itself. We do not participate in community entirely out of fear, i.e., out of a pragmatic need that makes us abject, reluctant participants in community. We are social beings whose lives are enriched by community, and we derive much of our sense of enjoyment, love and beauty from our community. Etzioni (1996, p. 26) states: "Social thinking has to cease viewing communal attachments as cannonballs chained to inmates' legs, needed to maintain their stability but 'encumbering.' The social fabric sustains, nourishes and enables individuality rather than diminishes it."

I can offer interpreters as an example. When I was starting out as an interpreter, I was very aware of my dependence upon other interpreters for support, for information, and for reinforcement in what I was doing in my new profession. Over the years, however, that sense of interdependence has developed into a sense of family. The fears of the unfamiliar have grown into the love of my work and of the people who do such work with me.

I also have become even more aware of my love of wild things, more concerned about protecting them, yet at the same time my love of the people who live in this landscape has grown. I find that I am more understanding when people act out of fear, when they fail to see wildlife the way I do, and even when they cause harm. The upshot of all this is my belief that in the community circle we begin with interdependence, but mature into love.

Beyond that center, the circle of community is completed with two axes (*Fig. 2*). One axis, which I describe as the Participation or Engagement axis, has responsibility and enjoyment at its two ends. For the community to survive and function, its members need to be willing to behave responsibly and contribute appropriately. Such mutual expressions of responsibility make it possible for us to draw our enjoyment, and all the things that we need, from the community.

Responsibility is a component of community which I regard as exclusively human. Other species appear to make their contributions to the community automatically, without hesitation. Only we humans appear to have sufficient free will to be responsible for our actions. We can make choices, and our choices can facilitate community existence or threaten it. At the same time, our numbers and technology have given us the power to damage the Earth greatly. For the community to be healthy, we individual humans need to accept responsibility for the effects of our actions on the community and choose to behave accordingly.

So far the community seems to be very serious---interesting, enriching perhaps, but sober. It seems to me, however, that *enjoyment* is an indispensable part of being a member of a community, at least for us humans. The rewards of living come through our interactions with other community members, be they human or non-human.

The other axis within the community circle I call the Respect axis. One end of this axis (particularization) focuses on the individual, recognizing the unique qualities and value contributed to the community by that member. The other end of the axis (inclusiveness) recognizes that all who enter the community space automatically are members of that community, and deserve to be respected as such.

Particularization emphasizes that a community is composed of individuals, each one different from all the others, each enlivening the community with a unique set of qualities, each contributing uniquely to community function. Respect for the value of each human being, of each plant and animal, and also respect for the self (self esteem) emerges from a grasp of this concept. Lack of respect leads to despair, anger, and environmental damage.

Inclusiveness is necessary to add warmth to the community. No one is excluded. The "unifying trait" that binds the members of the community I am describing is life, existence. So many of our problems arise because of our eagerness to divide the world into in-groups and out-groups. Racial, ethnic, economic and class lines are responsible for much suffering. Imagined separations between humans and "the environment," or "nature," endanger our survival: if we can imagine ourselves separate from the Earth, as our use of these words implies, then we can damage the Earth with impunity. An "environment" is like a stage set, replaceable and therefore expendable.

Inclusiveness does not lead necessarily to a single, Earth-wide community, bound by the biosphere. It seems to me that any geographic area could define a community's boundaries, as long as the people in that area retain a sense of pluralism. Indeed, it is difficult for me to imagine a community without reference to its particular, local landscape.

Perspective on Community

These ideas are not derived solely from my own theorizing and observing. I will mention two particular influences. First, I have studied descriptions of tradition-based societies from around the world, and conversed with people having ties to such societies, Native Americans especially. These sources account for my views on particularization, the inclusion of non-humans in the community (e.g., Hallowell 1975), the recognition of a human responsibility to the landscape (e.g., Nelson 1983), and interdependence.

A second major influence is social philosopher Amitai Etzioni (1991a,b; 1995, 1996) and colleagues, who have done a considerable amount of writing and speaking about "communitarianism" (I use quotation marks on the word because Etzioni does not use it as the dictionary does. Communally held property is not a part of Etzioni's meaning).

Etzioni's approach is sociological and political, an attempt to find a balance between the needs of the (human) community as a whole (expressed as an agreed upon "voluntary moral order") and the rights of individuals. This approach places communitarians at odds with civil libertarians, who maintain that the rights of individuals always must be given priority when they conflict with the needs of the community, no matter what is at stake, and with those who willingly would create an authoritarian state for the sake of an imagined security (see the Etzioni references for some thought-provoking examples). Etzioni advocates the forthright statement and expression of community enhancing values. Responsibility, interdependence and inclusiveness (in the form of human pluralism) play major roles on the moral order side of Etzioni's dynamic balance concept, and enjoyment and particularization on the individualistic side. As to the center, Etzioni (1996, p. 127) says, "[c]ommunity is defined by two characteristics: first, a web of affect-laden relationships among a group of individuals, relation-

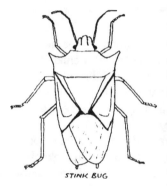
STINK BUG

ships that often crisscross and reinforce one another (rather than merely one-on-one or chainlike individual relationships), and second, a measure of commitment to a set of shared values, norms, and meanings, and a shared history and identity---in short, to a particular culture." Communitarians express concern that we Americans need to emphasize our common values while sharing and celebrating (but not overemphasizing) our ethnic diversity (Ravich 1995).

Importance of Community in Interpretation

Environmental problems such as pollution and abuse of the landscape, and social problems such as poverty, drug abuse and crime, have common roots in a failure to appreciate interdependence, a lack of respect for the value of the individual, a failure to accept all members of the community, an avoidance of responsibility, and the adoption of too grim an outlook. Interpreters can teach about community so as to help set the ground work for solving this broad range of problems. Social workers also could benefit by identifying and building the local community's sense of itself as a living entity within a living, supportive landscape, and especially by respecting the individual and her or his needs while teaching the other components of community.

Interpreters are doing excellent work in this area already. Two particularly good examples are Barton et al. (1992) and White (1991). The latter paper is a riveting read. White demonstrates the importance of respecting and sincerely caring about the people for whom we are interpreting. Those who are in pain need to start with respect for themselves and for others and we can respect and care about them even against their resistance. From that starting point we can proceed to responsibility and interdependence, and finally inclusiveness and enjoyment. But we have to model these things. This is interpretation because it begins from where the client is, which may be far removed from our desired endpoint. Our ultimate goal may be to bring people in touch with the Earth, but our success may be contingent on our acknowledging their more pressing needs first.

The Willowbrook Safari

I was putting together these ideas on community at the same time I was preparing to revise the self-guided tour for children's groups visiting the Willowbrook Wildlife Center. I decided to structure the grade 4-6 level of the program with the goals of teaching the community concept, and leading participants to an appreciation of their role within the community.

A group is met in our theater by a uniformed volunteer or staff member who wears a pith helmet and takes on the role of Walker or Wanda Wonderseeker, the Safari Master. Wonderseeker informs the group that they are going to go on a safari, a re-enactment of the original expedition which Wonderseeker led through this forest preserve years ago. Because it is a re-enactment, the children and their leaders will be playing the roles of members of the original safari team. Thus all the participants, not just the interpreter, become theatrical characters. For instance, Gottahava Holmes (Gottahav if the child is a boy) searches for nests, "Fingers" Malone touches tree bark, Lester or Lisa Little focuses on tiny things, Heinrich or Henrietta von Sixlegger seeks insects, etc. Walker spends 15-20 seconds focused fully on each child when assigning names and jobs. Each child is given a name tag like Walker's. They are instructed that as they make their discoveries, they are to share these with the other members of their safari team.

The adult group leader ("Lucky" Lookinfind) carries a map of the safari trail route and descriptions of activities to lead at different stops along the way. There are six stops, one for each of the elements of community, and a final stop which ties them all together. Instead of long, abstract words, the elements of community are identified through short sentences. For instance, the sign marking the stop for particularization is titled, "Each of us is different and important." One of the particularization teaching activities is to find two plants of the same kind and discover five difference between them.

The roles themselves express the components of community. Particularization appears as Walker assigns the various names and jobs, emphasizing the importance of each child. There is a hint of inclusiveness here, too, because everyone equally has a new name and task. Responsibility begins with the assignment to share discoveries, and interdependence results as children benefit from others' discoveries. A common behavior, unintended in the original program design, which also brings out the idea of interdependence, emerges when the children help one another with their jobs. Signs of enjoyment usually are evident from beginning to end. The various activities at the six stops are intended to make the components of community conscious and to provide diverse examples and applications, extending the community concept into the children's lives beyond the immediate safari experience.

Conclusion

What is the purpose of your interpretation? How broad is the vision and the responsibility you want to accept? Do you touch only some aspect of your constituents' lives with some aspect of your own, or are you a complete person in contact with other complete people? These are questions that we all answer in one way or another as we do our work and live our lives. Interpreters, in my experience are generalists and holists. I believe that we are capable of addressing our immediate interpretive goals within a broader context that goes beyond our site, and beyond our focus as interpretive naturalists or cultural interpreters. Whether or not you buy into the framework I have presented here, I hope you will consider the possibility that we can make our work relevant to all of society's needs. As teachers we do not have to save the world. We need only open people's eyes to the possibility that it can be saved, and point them in a direction that will make it so.

Chapter 1: Particularization

A grasshopper walked into a bar. The bartender said, "Hey, we have a drink named after you!"
The grasshopper said, "You have a drink named Bob?"

"When you can see each leaf as a separate thing, you can see the tree; when you can see the tree, you can see the spirit of the tree; when you can see the spirit of the tree you can talk to it and maybe begin to learn something." Yurok elder to Thomas Buckley (1979).

Defining Particularization

There is a temptation for interpreters to abandon specifics in our work. Science gives us theories about how nature functions, leading us to teach about ecosystem-level processes rather than about the unique features of each particular landscape and the flora and fauna within them. I believe that this temptation needs to be balanced with more of a focus on particulars. Particularization is the process of giving importance to individual landscape features (organisms, rocks, places), as well as to the individual persons for whom we interpret, and ourselves as individual interpreters.

Concepts and theories are helpful but they are artificial, human constructs. Have you ever seen a food chain? Oh, sure, you saw a kestrel nail a vole just last week. One kestrel. One vole. Food chains supposedly represent entire populations. They have little arrows. They appear static on paper but in the field we see nothing static. While the food chain concept is valid, it is an abstract generalization rather than a precise description of reality. Concepts can get in the way of an understanding of the nuts and bolts of nature.

Concepts are difficult to get excited about; we cannot see them. On the other hand...didn't your heart race as you watched that kestrel carry off that vole? The excitement of particularization is the excitement of participation. People respond to interpretation of the local landscape because subconsciously they realize that they are a part of it---they move through it every day. If I want to interpret the food chain idea, I remind my audience that they are sending carbon dioxide into the surrounding landscape with every breath. The plants around them are absorbing that carbon dioxide, and using it to hold the sun's light energy. Their energized breath will remain behind when they leave, powering the lives of the plants and animals surrounding them at that moment.

We lose so much when we think only in terms of concepts such as species, and fail to attend to the individual. A while ago, I was speaking to a large group of fifth graders when I caught a movement out of the corner of my eye (I was in wide-angle vision, of course; see the chapter on awareness). Two squirrels were tightroping a telephone wire,  and as they crossed behind me the members of my audience began to giggle and point. A teachable moment. But if I saw them only as gray squirrels there would be little of interest I could have said, perhaps a comment on their balancing ability. But I used the awareness technique of seeing purely, and noticed that the lead squirrel was an old female who had been nursing for several weeks---her nipples were swollen, the hairless skin was gray against the white fur of her belly. The trailing squirrel's lean, smooth body and slightly smaller size indicated that he had been born that spring. The story became clear. He was chasing her. She was trying to wean him. By attending to the particulars, I had a much better story to tell.

We have come to emphasize the Earth as a whole, speaking of large-scale patterns of energy flow, climate, the effects of tropical deforestation and upper-atmosphere ozone erosion, and CO_2

buildup on the whole globe. These ideas are important and need attention. But let's not forget the local landscape. A few years back I wrote an article for the weekly newspaper of Culver, the little northern Indiana town where I grew up. The article described the local pre-settlement landscape and included a map, which I had drawn after studying the original land survey records and the county soils map. People were interested in all the little details about the origins of familiar landscape features. For instance, the dominant feature along the shoreline of Lake Maxinkuckee, the large glacial lake on which Culver is located, is Long Point. Long Point is oriented along a SW-NE axis, and that is not coincidental. It formed when sand was blown by prevailing winds from the nearby Tippecanoe River, originally a drainage route for glacial meltwater (Johnson et al. 1965). The sand was the most wear-resistant component of granite the glacier dragged down from Canada. I agree with Lutz (1985): "Out of the particularized experience and understanding of our own unique places...grow personally meaningful relationships with personally significant environments."

Perspectives on Particularization

Traditional societies throughout the world use local landscape features in their teaching stories. The Dreamtime legends of the Australian aborigines include origins for certain rock formations and water holes, lending a concreteness to myth. Basso (1986) tells how Apache elders use stories to "stalk" the young. A misbehaving child is included in a group being told a story about the unpleasant consequences bestowed upon someone who misbehaved in a similar way. The story is tied to a particular stone, river bend or other landscape feature. The child is not reprimanded directly--- he or she figures out the lesson, corrects the behavior, and for the rest of his or her life the landscape feature is a constant reminder of the proper behavior.

I remain unimpressed by the interpretive practice of shunning labels for the entities of nature. Sure, it's poor practice to point to a tree, say "Kentucky coffee tree," and move on. But it's even worse to pretend that all the trees are the same. Each species has unique and interesting biological features. The combinations of tree species we see in today's forests are completely different from the mixes that existed under different climatic conditions in the past (Davis 1989). This ecological fact underlines the importance of each species and gives perspective to the community concept. Furthermore, each species has had its own significance to man for medicine, for food, or for building. Kentucky coffee trees are legumes, enriching the soil as beans do through mutualistic partnership with nitrogen-fixing bacteria. Male and female flowers are on separate trees---this is a plant with a clear sexual identity. The leaves are doubly compound, which means that much of the supportive structure for photosynthetic tissue is dropped in the fall, giving the tree its peculiarly sparse, dead look in winter. The seeds were used by Native Americans and pioneers to prepare a beverage. Two of the more unusual medicinal uses were a last-resort enema for terminal cases of constipation, and a bark preparation used to bring people out of comas by inducing uncontrollable sneezing fits (Gilmore 1977). These are stories which people want to hear. They exist for every species.

And don't stop with the species. Honor the differences among individuals. A tree tells its story in the details of its structure and scars, and the story is different from that of the conspecific tree growing beside it.

As you learn more about the particulars of a landscape, there is a point at which they begin to fuse together to form an integrated whole. An animal, a plant or a footprint has its complete meaning only in context. At the same time it contains clues about the landscape around it, just as the structure of a small piece of a mineral or a single cell from an organism contains essential information about the whole. Lopez (1978) gives a sense of this: "On a riverbank, for example, faced with a few wolf tracks headed in a certain direction, perhaps a scent mark, the Nunamiut will call on his own knowledge of this area (as well as his knowledge of wolves, what time of year it is, and so on) and on things he has heard from others and make an educated guess at what this particular cluster of clues might mean---which wolves these might have been, where they were headed, why, how long ago, and so on."

Particularization in Interpretation

Every person for whom we interpret needs something a little different from us. Some wish to be informed, some to be entertained. Some just want a little attention, while others want to pretend that they are spectating from afar. Some are seekers who don't really know why they came, others are there because someone else made them come. Each person has a unique learning style, and a group of any size will contain individuals with conflicting learning and thinking styles.

The concept of left- and right-brain thinking could have opened people's minds to differences in learning style, made them more tolerant of others and more flexible. Unfortunately the L-R model is too simple to describe human variation adequately for practical purposes such as teaching. Furthermore, it is a polarity and thus tempts people to judge whether "L" or "R" is better. More suitable systems of learning styles will be elaborated in a later chapter.

There are limits to what an interpreter can do when faced with a group of strangers for a short time. But we can do some things. We can be alert for opportunities to speak to individuals. We can try to give each person a sense that we are giving individualized teaching and attention. If we notice the small feedback signals they give us, we learn which ones need more of this closeness and which ones need more distance. We can listen to our gut feelings about individuals. Sometimes sullenness in a child is a defense mechanism that begins to crumble as soon as we show that we care, that we want him or her to be involved. There is much promise in research such as Brenda Lackey's (1997) that looks at the moment-to-moment responses by audience members to interpretive presentations.

We plant many seeds as interpreters. We are role models. By showing people that we care for them as individuals, we can make ourselves significant in their memory, and maybe part of what they absorb or try to imitate in us is our love of the Earth. And after all, if we really love the Earth, we love every part, which includes ourselves and every person we meet.

Now for a blending of the particular landscape with the particular interpreter. The place in which you interpret has to be selected so that it will blend with your spirit and the intent of your interpretation. Even if you don't accept the notion that a place has a spirit of its own, you know that you like some places better than others. By all means uses this information when you decide where you will do your interpreting.

It should be clear from all of this that I am not in agreement with those who place the emphasis on the education program, assuming the individual teacher or interpreter is an interchangeable automaton. Canned programs are like fast food. There is some nourishment there, and certainly it's better than nothing. But no program is good enough to function alone. No program, no matter how complete the detail of its design, will succeed unless it can be bent---a lot---to fit the teacher, the students, the place and the circumstances. I like the way interpreter Mike Miller of Peoria puts it (December 1989, *pers. comm.*): "I know how tempting it is for an aspiring interpreter to fall in love with a 'canned program'. I fell into that trap when first starting out. I soon realized that the use of many of these programs was like putting a gag on Mother Nature. The medium of the program often becomes the message. The Earth speaks very quietly to people, and these programs often equip the participants with blinders and earplugs." Every teacher is important for what he or she brings to that human interaction with a student. And the most important component of the teacher's attitude is love.

Conclusion

One final point. So often I hear expressions of despair from people who understand the serious trouble the Earth is in. They are overwhelmed by the job of saving her. Just remember that you are not alone---your job is not to save the whole Earth. You have a particular role to play, a particular job to do. Plant your own seeds, leave the rest for others, and don't let your worries impede you. The following story, my own retelling of a well-known tale, seems relevant to the subject of particularization. This version is a combination of several sources along with my own twists (sources are Quigley 1959, Saxe 1963, Shah 1967, Backstein 1992, Geri Collard pers. com. 1997, Merrill Kohlhofer pers. com. 1997, and Young [publication date unknown]). And, please, recognize that the "blindness" referenced in this story is metaphoric. It is not a superficial reference to physically blind people.

The Blind Men and the Elephant

In the farthest reaches of the desert there was a city in which all the people were blind. A king and his army were passing through that region, and camped outside the city. The king had with him a great elephant, which he used for heavy work and to frighten his enemies in battle. The people of the city had heard of elephants, but never had the opportunity to know one. Out rushed 6 young men, determined to discover what the elephant was like.

The first young man, in his haste, ran straight into the side of the elephant. He spread out his arms and felt the animal's broad, smooth side. He sniffed the air, and thought, "This is an animal, my nose leaves no doubt of that, but this animal is like a wall." He rushed back to the city to tell of his discovery.

The second young blind man, feeling through the air, grasped the elephant's trunk. The elephant was surprised by this, and snorted loudly. The young man, startled in turn, exclaimed, "This elephant is like a snake, but it is so huge that its hot breath makes a snorting sound." He turned to run back to the city and tell his tale.

The third young blind man walked into the elephant's tusk. He felt the hard, smooth ivory surface of the tusk, listened as it scraped through the sand, then as the elephant lifted the tusk out, he could feel its pointed tip. "How wonderful!" he thought. "The elephant is hard and sharp like a spear, and yet it makes noises and smells like an animal!" Off he ran.

The fourth young blind man reached low with his hands, and found one of the elephant's legs. He reached around and hugged it, feeling its rough skin. Just then, the elephant stomped that foot, and the man let go. "No wonder this elephant frightens the king's enemies," he thought. "It is like a tree trunk or a mighty column, yet it bends, is very strong, and strikes the ground with great force." Feeling a little frightened himself, he fled back to the city.

The fifth young blind man found the elephant's tail. "I don't see what all the excitement is about," he said. "The elephant is nothing but a frayed bit of rope." He dropped the tail and ran after the others.

The sixth young blind man was in a hurry, not wanting to be left behind. He heard and felt the air as it was pushed by the elephant's flapping ear, then grasped the ear itself and felt its thin roughness. He laughed with delight. "This wonderful elephant is like a living fan." And, like the others, he was satisfied with his quick first impression and headed back to the city.

But finally, an old blind man came. He had left the city, walking in his usual slow way, content to take his time and study the elephant thoroughly. He walked all around the elephant, touching every part of it, smelling it, listening to all of its sounds. He found the elephant's mouth and fed the animal a treat, then petted it on its great trunk. Finally he returned to the city, only to find it in an uproar. Each of the six young men had acquired followers who eagerly heard his story. But then, as the people found that there were six different contradictory descriptions, they all began to argue. The old man quietly listened to the fighting. "It's like a wall!" "No, it's like a snake!" "No, it's like a spear!" "No, it's like a tree!" "No, it's like a rope!" "No, it's like a fan!"

The old man turned and went home, laughing as he remembered his own foolishness as a young man. Like these, he once hastily concluded that he understood the whole of something when he had experienced only a part. He laughed again as he remembered his greater foolishness of once being unwilling to discover truth for himself, depending wholly on others' teachings. But he laughed hardest of all as he realized that he had become the only one in the city who did not know what an elephant is like.

Chapter 2: Responsibility

For example, among certain families there is a great emphasis on table manners, a very definite etiquette. Nothing much is said: a young one watches and learns. When it is old enough to know right from wrong but still misbehaves at meals, its meal-basket is turned over, upside down. Hungry or not, no more food. It's up to the child to figure out what's wrong and to fix it, and thus to start learning about the laws concerning food and the respect for both resources and other human beings that underlie them. (from an article on Yurok education methods, Buckley 1979).

Defining Responsibility

The avoidance of responsibility for one's actions has become an art form. The legal profession has been built largely on the foundation of blaming others for one's troubles. "You are responsible" is heard much more often than "I am responsible."

Responsibility can be indirect and unclear. The most common cause of injury to young wild animals brought to the hospital at the Willowbrook Wildlife Center is attacks by free-running pet cats and dogs. Who is responsible for those injuries? Assigning responsibility to any of the animals involved is problematic. To expect a vulnerable young wild animal to avoid such an attack, or to expect a pet animal with the instincts of its wild ancestors to restrain from behaving accordingly, is unrealistic. Yet, a conscious choice was made in this matter by the people who acted to release the pet to run freely. The responsibility for the attack is theirs.

Taking Full Responsibility

What is the opposite of responsibility? If nothing that I am, and nothing that happens to me, and nothing that I do, is my responsibility, then what is left of me? I am no more a person than is a beer bottle, to be emptied and tossed or, if the drinker is responsible, recycled. The opposite attitude, of accepting full responsibility for my life, can have profound personal implications. Suppose I accept the belief that I am fully responsible not only for what I do, but for what I am and even for what happens to me? This means that I have to act consciously, considering all the consequences I can imagine, and realize my creative role in those consequences. Does the highway litterer do this? Accepting full responsibility for what I am means that if I don't like some aspect of myself, I must take the steps to change and grow. I have to abandon the easy outs of blaming others and seeing myself as a victim. This is no small step. It requires courage, and some of the side effects can be painful. But if I don't like some aspect of myself, who is more responsible for making the required changes than I am?

Taking responsibility for what happens to me is more complex. It seems counterintuitive at first. It requires looking at the world in an unconventional way. It means looking realistically at my life and the choices I have made and continue to make. I cannot consciously control everything that happens to me, but I can look to those areas I can control and make better choices. What can I do differently to prevent unpleasant experiences from arising? Covey (1989) refers to this as the Circle of Influence, the areas in my life that I can control or guide, and promotes a proactive approach. Attitudes and fears seem to play a big part: my fears often seem to attract what I fear, as though some unconscious part of myself guides me into the confrontation as a necessary growth step. Similarly, an unshakeable positive attitude often seems to warp the world around it to conform to itself. I believe that optimists and pessimists both are right, and both are actively involved in creating the worlds in which they live. The trap in this manner of thinking is that it can lead me to blame myself for my illnesses, setbacks and other misfortunes. The trick is to see them not as misfortunes but as opportunities, necessary steps in the process. I take responsibility for them, embrace them, learn from them.

Here is how Deepak Chopra (1994, p. 58) puts it: "When you feel frustrated or upset by a person or a situation, remember that you are not reacting to the person or the situation, but to your feelings about the person or the situation. These are your feelings, and your feelings are not someone else's fault. When you recognize and understand this completely, you are ready to take responsibility for how you feel and to change it. And if you can accept things as they are, you are ready to take responsibility for your situation and for all the events you see as problems." Note how similar this statement is to Covey's (1989, p.73): "It's not what happens to us, but our response to what happens to us that hurts us. Of course, things can hurt us physically or economically and can cause sorrow. But our character, our basic identity, does not have to be hurt at all. In fact, our most difficult experiences become the crucibles that forge our character and develop the internal powers, the freedom to handle difficult circumstances in the future and to

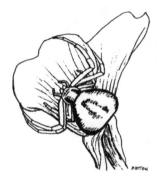

inspire others to do so as well." Malone and Malone (1987, p. 106) use the term "reciprocity" to describe this unconventional view of the world: "Reciprocity means that we are all actively involved in what happens to us; no one is the singular and ultimate villain. There is no such simplistic format as cause and effect in relationships...Nature knows no unconnected realities. In minor or major ways, everyone is involved. Reciprocity is not either your causing X and my being affected by X, or the reverse; it is us together. Whatever is happening to us is happening to me; whatever is happening to me is happening to us."

The Shadow

All this self examination revolves around the concept of the shadow (Zweig and Abrams 1991), the notion that we are complete beings who have buried parts of ourselves, some parts "good" and others "evil." When we reconcile ourselves with that shadow we are comfortable with ourselves and capable of being fully responsible. The alternative is to deny our darker parts, projecting them onto others, getting disproportionately emotional in our blame and hatreds, putting responsibility on others while avoiding our own. When we deny the brighter parts of shadow we are filled with admiration, envy and longing. By acknowledging and then containing the dark parts of our shadow selves, and by noticing and then developing the bright parts, we can understand ourselves and others better, grow in all ways, and accept full responsibility for ourselves and our lives.

One of my favorite legends from Europe addresses responsibility, while also commenting on the shadow. My version of that legend follows (based on Hudleston 1965, Armstrong 1973, Green 1985, and versions by Robert Wilhelm and Chris Lee-Thompson).

The Wolf of Gubbio

During the middle ages of Europe, nations as we know them today did not exist. They were a new and developing invention. People identified more with the city they lived in or near, and cities had to provide many of the things we look to nations to provide today. Among these things was the common defense, and cities were known to attack one another. As a result, cities in those days were walled and fortress like. There were only a few breaks in the walls for roads, and heavy gates could be closed. The wall represented a boundary between the city and the broad world. Gubbio was a city in central Italy, and Gubbio was surrounded by a such a wall.

Early in the 13th Century a shadow emerged from the forest at Gubbio. I say a shadow, because at first no one saw it and lived to describe it. Its fangs and weight took down both livestock and men, and its long legs carried it back into the forest, gray fur and bushy tail vanishing before the remains of its victims were discovered. Perhaps you have correctly guessed that this shadow was in fact a large wolf. Free-running wolves in North America have not been known to prey on human beings, but a few cases are known from Europe, and Gubbio's time of terror in the early 13th Century is one of those.

Death was more of an everyday occurrence then than it is now. But as the deaths mounted, people became frightened. The fright grew to near panic after two young men armed with swords went out hunting the wolf and later were found killed, their swords still in their scabbards. The gates were closed, and people were very reluctant to venture outside Gubbio's ancient fortifications.

Word of Gubbio's troubles spread throughout the region. A monk in a nearby town heard the story. This monk had gained a reputation for his modesty, his vows of poverty, and his love both of people and of animals. Having heard about this wolf, the monk felt that he should go to Gubbio. The people of Gubbio welcomed him as he spent some time there assessing the situation. But as his plans to leave the town and venture into the forest became known, the people urged him not to go. This wolf was surely too monstrous for anyone to confront. Besides, the people feared, if the beloved monk were killed trying to aid them, the reputation of Gubbio would be ruined. But the monk refused to be dissuaded. He passed through the gate, went out beyond the wall, and took the road to the forest. When he reached the trees a howl rose up from the depths of the woods.

It is said that the monk felt his way toward the heart of the darkness, there in the forest. This seems a fanciful exaggeration. Yet in time he and the wolf found and faced one another. The wolf opened its jaws widely as it prepared to leap. But the monk stood firm, made a sign of the cross, and said two words only: "Brother Wolf." What happened next is not certain, for the various versions of this legend disagree. They come back into concordance later, however, agreeing that the monk emerged from the forest with the wolf walking at his side.

Toward town they walked, the monk and the wolf together. They walked through the gates and into the city. The wolf was within the walls! Monk and wolf moved on, past shocked towns-people, and word spread like lightning. Crowds of people converged upon Gubbio's central plaza, where the two appeared to be heading. The immense Piazza della Signoria looks out over a large part of Gubbio, as the city is on the slope of a mountainside, and you can see all the way out to the walls from there.

The monk and wolf arrived, moved to a place in the center, and the crowd grew quiet as the man prepared to speak. But all he said was this: "People of Gubbio. This wolf your brother was starving. Hunger made him behave as he did. People of Gubbio. Here is what you must do. You must feed your wolf."

There was a moment of shocked silence. Surely he would have more to say than this. But when it became clear that he was done, the plaza suddenly filled with discussion and argument. "Our wolf? What does he mean, our wolf? We didn't ask for this wolf. We don't want this wolf." And in fact there was a common practice in those days to hang wolves by the neck from ropes, like human criminals. But some people looked at the wolf, trying to see it as the monk saw it. They saw its emaciated condition, the ribs standing out individually. They saw it as it was, a beautiful creature reduced by injury or age or illness to a weakened state where it no longer could make its living by preying on wild animals. Others were influenced by this monk, by his reputation and example, and by the wonderful miracle they had witnessed in their town. So to everyone's surprise there emerged a consensus that the people would feed their wolf. Their wolf! Who would have thought it?

Thus the people of Gubbio made peace with their wolf. The animal lived for two more years. People fed him with great pleasure as he went from door to door. No dog barked at him. He died of old age, and he was greatly mourned. The walls of Gubbio suddenly seemed very empty.

As for the monk, he was destined to achieve sainthood and worldwide fame, back there in his own home town of Assissi.

(Note: I like that story, though I would never advise people to feed any wildlife other than songbirds in winter. But this is a story built largely out of metaphors, and a broad view of responsibility clearly is one of its lessons.)

Chapter 3: Inclusiveness

As far as anyone can tell, no species other than ours judges the value or desirability of other species in the community. This is realistic: to ignore a newly arrived species or get hung up in values concerning it would distract community members so as to threaten their welfare. We see this on small islands, where newly introduced predators often have devastated endemic species that had lost the ability to recognize or respond to such a predator.

We, on the other hand, are quick to make judgements about our communities and what individuals or species should or should not be permitted in them. (Granted, sometimes our influences on biological communities have made such judgements necessary). Some of us are quick to fight over minor differences in religion or ethnic background. As in the last chapter, I would like to turn this question on its head and ask, why are we not inclusive? And, just as that approach to responsibility leads us to consider the unexpected consequences of our actions, so does a close examination of inclusiveness lead to an unexpected focus on the concept of forgiveness.

Poison ivy has a lesson to teach regarding inclusiveness, I think. The most common question I get about poison ivy, other than how to identify it, is this: what good is it? Behind that question is the assumption that living beings have value only in relation to us. Such an assumption leads naturally to the conclusion that if something is detrimental to us, it has no value and in fact the Universe would be better off without it. There are two levels of answer one could give to this question. The more straightforward, simpler answer is to point out a couple of concrete things poison ivy does which most would agree are "good." The most straightforward lesson taught by poison ivy is awareness. The possibility of touching the plant and getting a rash encourages people to keep their eyes open, paying attention to their surroundings in the woods and not taking them for granted. Poison ivy also could be used as a metaphor for connectedness. Poison ivy is a vine, but does not always appear to be one. Sometimes it climbs trees, but sometimes its main stem runs just below the surface of the ground, sending up shoots at intervals which on the surface appear to be separate plants, but in fact are united, a single entity. In the realm of more concrete benefits, there is one recorded medicinal use I have found for the plant: a poultice of the leaves sometimes was used to open boils (King 1984). Also, at least in northeastern Illinois, poison ivy is by far the most important food plant for deer and cottontail rabbits in February. Most people like deer and bunny rabbits, so this answer makes poison ivy "good" in their minds.

After getting this far, sometimes I am asked the follow-up question: how can some animals eat poison ivy without getting the rash? The answer brings us to the topic of forgiveness. It turns out that poison ivy does not produce the rash alone. Urushiol, the resin that we pick up from poison ivy, contains phenolic components that react with skin proteins, and it is the resulting product that stimulates us to produce the rash (Lampe and McCann 1985, Turner and Szczawinski 1991). People who lack that allergen-producing capacity in their skin (15-50% of us) don't get the reaction. Poison ivy alone does not cause the rash: we are equal contributors. When we blame poison ivy we are forgetting that it is our own choice to go into its domain, to touch it, and it turns out that we contribute half of the chemical components that lead to the rash. Recognition of our act of projection is a step on the road to true forgiveness, and opens the way to inclusiveness. If we get the rash, can we honestly blame the plant? And if we cannot blame it, can we honestly exclude it from the community?

Notice how this topic, like that of responsibility, leads us to the shadow and thereby back to ourselves. We are, after all, typically selective in our forgiveness. A small child in play stumbles into me. He still is learning to control his body, he clearly intended no harm, and if I had been more alert I could have avoided the collision. I forgive easily, forget instantly. True forgiveness is strange and unconventional to our thinking, because in it the "offense" might as well never have happened, for all the thought we give to it afterwards. It is this form of forgiveness that admits poison ivy to the community, and forms the foundation of inclusiveness.

Malone and Malone (1987, p. 73) point out that acceptance may be the more appropriate concept than forgiveness at the personal level: "When we feel accepted even though disagreed with, we do not feel tolerated; we feel loved...Acceptance has nothing to do with judgment. With acceptance, there is no better or worse, healthier or sicker, mature or immature. Acceptance has to do with differences without judgment. You are different from me, but I experience you as neither better nor worse than I am. Just different from me. And that difference does not separate us."

Another of my favorite lessons in inclusiveness is the following story. My retelling is based mainly on a Cherokee version from Mooney (1902), but also on the Muskogee variant relayed by Bruchac (1994) with, as usual, twists of my own.

The Ball Game of the Birds and the Mammals

Long ago, when animals could talk and lived much as people do now, the mammals and the birds had a quarrel. The birds said, "We are better than you because we have wings." The mammals said, "We are better than you because we have teeth." Then Eagle, leader of the birds, suggested, "Let us have a ball game. The first team to score a goal wins the argument, and gets to be champion of the animal world." Bear, leader of the mammals, agreed.

The two teams separated to have their pre-ballgame dances. The birds flew up to the top of the tree-covered mountain overlooking the meadow where the game would take place. The birds all danced to show how they would play the game. There were the fluttering birds like Cardinal and Blue Jay, the gliding birds like Purple Martin and Whip-poor-will, and the soaring birds like Eagle and Tla'nua the hawk.

Meanwhile, the mammals were dancing down in the meadow. Bear was throwing great logs about, showing his strength and bragging: "Any beakface that tries to take the ball from me will wish he never left his egg." And the deer was running swiftly, showing his great speed. Some of the smaller birds were frightened by Bear's threat, but soon the dancing was over and the birds began to preen their feathers so they would look their best in the game.

Now, about this time, along came two little animals, hardly bigger than mice. They climbed all the way up to the top of that mountain, and found the tree where Eagle was perched. Then they climbed up that tree until they reached the branch where the leader of the birds was preening his feathers. They edged out on the branch. One of them said, "Oh, great Eagle..." The other little animal interrupted him and said, "Louder!" "OH, GREAT EAGLE, could we be on your team?"

Eagle looked at those little animals with his one eye, the way birds will, and said, "You have teeth. You belong on the team down there in the meadow."

"We tried to be on their team, but they laughed at us and said we were too small. Then they tried to step on us and chased us away."

Eagle took pity on the little animals, and said, "Why, of course you may be on our team, but how can you play with the birds when you have no wings?"

Now, all the other birds had been listening. Crow and Blue Jay, who are the cleverest of birds, spoke up and said, "We think we have the answer. We need the drum." They took the drum from the dance and trimmed off all the little bits of leather around the edges. They made some splints out of the giant cane, and sewed together a pair of little leather wings, which they tied onto the front legs of the first little animal. He looked so different that he

needed to have a new name. They called him Tla'meha, at least, that is his Cherokee name. We know him as Bat. Eagle tossed the ball to Bat, and he flew with the most amazing flight, dodging and turning, twisting and doubling back. The birds realized that this would be one of their best players.

But now, what would they do about the other little animal? They had used all the leather they could spare from the drum; there was none left. Now Great Blue Heron and the stately white Egret spoke up. "We believe we have the answer. See how the skin is loose along the sides of that animal. We will stretch it out even more until he has, not wings, but at least a gliding skin he can stretch out." And so those two tall wading birds, each big enough to swallow that little animal with a gulp, landed on either side of him, reached down with their spearlike bills, picked him up by the two sides and pulled and pulled and stretched that skin, and pulled and pulled and stretched that skin, until he had flaps of gliding skin that stretched from wrist to ankle on each side. He, too, needed a new name and they called him Tewa. We know him as Flying Squirrel. The ball was tossed into the air and Tewa leaped after it, seized it in his teeth, stretched out his legs and began the long glide down the mountain. Down, down, far down he sailed, just above the treetops, leveled out at the bottom, zoomed over the heads of the startled mammal team, and landed on a tree on the far side of the meadow. He looked back the long way he had come, and saw in a great colorful cloud, fluttering and gliding and soaring, all the members of the birds' team, following him down the mountain. The time for the great game had come.

Two posts were set up at either end of the meadow. These would serve as the goals. The ball was tossed out and brave little Tewa, the Flying Squirrel, was so excited by his first gliding flight down the mountain that he leaped up and grabbed the ball in his teeth. He fell right back down, though, and now he had to run for his life because all the bigger mammals were trying to stomp on him. He ran like a brown streak to the edge of the meadow, climbed up a tree, then jumped and glided across, passing the ball on to Whip-poor-will. Whip-poor-will flashed his long wings and called out his hunting cry, then gave the ball to Cardinal. Cardinal did not have a big mouth like Whip-poor-will, and so bounced the ball off his back. The land animals ran beneath him, hoping he'd miss, and in fact he did bounce it too far to reach. The mammals stretched up for it, but down swooped Tla'nua the Hawk and seized it in his talons. Now Tla'nua taunted the mammals, making fun of them while he kept the ball just out of their reach. Then he passed the ball on to Eagle. The chief of the birds was much too dignified to do anything but soar above the meadow holding the ball. But he was wise enough to not keep all the attention for himself for long. Eagle gave the ball to Crow, who passed it to Jay, who turned it over to Heron, who passed it to Egret, who gave it to Duck, who dropped it.

The ball bounced once and was still on the ground. So hypnotized were the mammals by the interweaving flight of the birds that they did not move for a few seconds. Then the spell was broken as Bear leaped forward with a roar and reached for the ball. If he got it, with his strength he would keep it. It looked like the mammals would win. Bear was reaching out his claws to take the ball. But just then, down swooped that dark swallow, the Purple Martin. And just as Martin flies low over the water, dipping his head to take a drink, now he flew low above the meadow grasses, dipped his head, took the ball and flew right up between the outstretched arms of Bear. And now Martin turned to the birds' secret weapon. He gave the ball to Bat. Now, do you think that Bat kept safely out of reach of the mammals, as the birds had done? No, he did not. He flew straight at Bear. Bear saw him coming and began to swing his claws to swat him. But Bat sped up and flew around the bear, who was enraged but could not touch him. Then Bat flew at the swift-running Deer. But Deer had to stop, because no matter how fast he ran Bat flew faster, in an interweaving flight around and between Deer's legs. Bat left Deer behind and Bat, who the mammals had rejected, carried the ball through the goal and won the game for the birds.

The high honors went to Purple Martin, who risked his life to save the ball for the birds. He was given a gourd for his nest, and ever since then purple martins have preferred to nest in homes given to them by others. As for Bat and Flying Squirrel, they decided to keep their wings and gliding skin, so that all who see them will be reminded of the role they played in the ball game of the birds and mammals.

That ends the story. I find that children like it very much, and I suspect the reason is the important roles played by the small animals. It can be an empowering myth for a small child. The story has relevance to me, the adult, as well. What part of me does the bat represent? Can I be stronger by recognizing and accepting that part? Who are the bats in my world? Who do I not want to have on my team? Perhaps I should reconsider.

Chapter 4: Enjoyment

Follow your bliss. Joseph Campbell (1988, p. 91)

"Why didn't God simply provide a direct path to Himself?" Arthur asked.
"He did. Desire is the direct path, for there is no quicker way to God than your own wishes and needs. Why should God give you something before you want it?" Deepak Chopra (1995, p. 132)

I celebrate with horned toads and ravens and lizards and quail... And, Friend, it's not a bad party. Byrd Baylor (1986)

It's easy to fall prey to the temptation to take things seriously. Taking oneself too seriously is one of the great tragedies. It misleads us away from one of the greatest guides we have: enjoyment. We know this as children, most of us. We love to learn, until we are affected by the regimentation of a bad school experience or by peer pressures, and abandon the joy of learning. As a child, I loved the study of natural history more than anything. I pursued it episodically. For a couple of months I would be addicted to birds, would spend all my waking hours thinking about them, reading about them, watching them, listening to them. Then I would switch to astronomy. Then rocks and minerals, or insects, or reptiles and amphibians, or trees, or stamps (it wasn't *all* natural history, just most of it), back to birds, then chess, and so on. Where did this enthusiasm come from? In part it was from the outdoor orientation of my family (mainly toward hunting and fishing), in part from experiences like the ones I described in the book's introduction. Part of it was me, though. As a child I had blue eyes, blond hair and a love of nature study. I wasn't born with nature knowledge, but I was born with a strong capacity to want to acquire it.

There is a push and pull of inner desires that leads us to pursue our skills and interests. This enjoyment, this fiercely joyous drive, is the critical thing that develops talent. Brian is my 10-year-old neighbor. Someday people will call Brian a "natural athlete." He will be one of those who try out a new sport and perform at a high level the first time out. People will assume he has superior eye-hand coordination, reflexes, spatial awareness, and so forth, and they will be right, but what counts is not those things but rather his love of movement, his love of the game, whatever it is. Brian's always out there, bouncing a basketball, playing street hockey, joining the older kids for a game of baseball played with a tennis ball (which I appreciate because home runs often bounce off my roof or come close to my windows). Many's the time I've driven home to empty streets with a cold rain pouring down. Empty, that is, until I reach my block and see Brian out in the street playing with a soccer ball, soaking wet, with a look of concentrated joy on his face.

Brian is most completely engaged, however, when he is playing these games with others. He is vocal, he is demanding, but mostly he simply is the best. I have tried to think of a valid counterexample, but without success: enjoyment is always within a community context. We are interacting with other people, with parts of the landscape, in concrete or abstracted form, when we are experiencing enjoyment. Brian's games all are team sports. My pursuit of nature knowledge connected me with the broader community of the landscape. The stereotypic computer nerd, alone in a room, is connected through the Internet to millions. Enjoyment is a fundamental component of community, and a demonstration of the importance of community to us. So, the following story, from my own experience as a graduate student, is just for fun.

John and the Evinrude

There are no roads in western Alaska, where I spent four summers doing research in wildlife ecology. There are no roads, but there is a network of rivers and tidal sloughs which people can travel on boats pushed by outboard motors in summertime. This is the story of one such motor.

It was an Evinrude, an ancient, 40-horsepower, Evinrude outboard motor. It had lost its cover long ago, so that its gears and wheels and motor guts were exposed to the four winds. Up on top of it all was the big flywheel, the flywheel which spins to keep the motor turning smoothly through its cycles as it runs. And it is the flywheel around which the starting cord is wound, so that when you pull it the motor should start. Only, the original starting cord had broken off this motor long ago. So now all there was, was an old piece of rope with a knot on the end which you placed in a notch in the flywheel, then wound the rope around and around the flywheel, gripped the nail tied in the other end, pulled to spin the flywheel, and the rope came completely off so that when the motor didn't start you had to take the rope and wind it around the flywheel again. Did I say *when* the motor didn't start? On average it took 63 pulls to get that old Evinrude to run. And they were no small pulls, either, not on that big motor.

Well, you might wonder, why would we bother with a motor like that? Part of the answer is that motors are scarce and expensive in western Alaska, and if one can be made to go, it is used. However, it is true that we had other motors at our disposal. Smaller motors. The rest of the answer is that that Evinrude had power. When you put that motor on the back of your boat, it took you upriver so fast that you quickly made up for any time you lost in starting it.

One day we were going on a goose banding drive well up the Kokechik River. So we mounted the 40-horse Evinrude and ran up to a promising looking riverbend. We unloaded all our gear and prepared our trap: two long fences of netting, meeting to form a V, with a little corral at that junction where the geese would be driven. You see, geese and other waterfowl lose all their flight feathers for a couple of weeks in late summer. During that time you can herd them like little feathered, two-legged cattle. You can band them and take measurements from them. We had had several good banding drives in the previous two weeks, and we figured this would probably be the last one of the season.

We hiked across the soggy tundra, then spread out to form a line about a mile out from the open V of the trap. When everyone was ready we started to slog back through the ponds and marshes and tundra toward the fences, waving our raincoats in the air and yelling like fools. The drive wasn't great. About 15 emperor and cackling Canada geese moved up ahead of us. They waddled up to the net, looked at us, looked at the net . . . and then spread their wings and flew right out of the trap.

Well, the banding season clearly was over. We ate lunch, took down the trap, loaded it into the boat, and it was time to start the Evinrude and head back to camp. It was my turn to start the Evinrude.

The others all sat down in the boat. I took my place on the back seat, and checked the choke and other settings. It soon became clear that we had a complication in starting the motor this time. A strong wind had come up from the west and was pushing the boat against the shore, where the river was too shallow to lower the propeller into the water.

So one of the two Daves took out the oar and pushed the boat out from shore. For some reason it was an unwritten rule in the Fish and Wildlife Service to keep one, and only one oar in each camp. You can't row a boat with one oar. All it will do is spin in a circle in one place. You can't paddle a boat with an oar, it's too long and awkward for that. The best you can do is to use it as a push pole. But an oar makes a lousy push pole. The narrow blade sinks deep into the sticky soft gray silt that covers the bottom of every river and slough in western Alaska. So for every three feet that Dave pushed us forward with the oar, he pulled us back two feet getting the oar blade out of the silt.

Finally the boat was in deep enough water that I could lower the motor into the water, wind the cord around the flywheel, and make the first pull. This I did, and of course the motor didn't start, it was only the first pull. By then, the wind had us up against the shore again, so Dave took the oar and pushed us out again. It took us twenty minutes to get the first 15 pulls.

Finally someone thought to throw out the anchor. It would hold us off shore until we got the motor going, and we wouldn't lose so much time push-poling with the darned oar. Now I could concentrate on winding and pulling, winding and pulling. Thirty pulls passed, forty, sixty. Every once in a while the motor would cough or sputter a little, just enough to encourage me, but I was getting tired. Seventy pulls. I was taking more and more time between pulls, getting very tired.

Finally, after the 73rd pull, John offered to take over. John was a Canadian grad student, a black-bearded pipe-smoker, and John was smooth. I have never met a better liar, or teller of impromptu tall tales. John prided himself on his ability to deal with people and with reluctant outboard motors. As we exchanged places, John confidently predicted that he would start the Evinrude within 5 pulls.

This made things interesting. It wasn't that we had a bet on. No wager was needed. John already had staked his pride and reputation, and that was enough to make it interesting to us. He checked all the settings, the choke and the throttle, wrapped the cord around the flywheel, and gave a mighty pull. But nothing happened. He wound the cord a second time and pulled. Nothing. He wound the cord again, patted the engine on its side. Pulled. Nothing. Wound the cord again. This time he patted the flywheel. Pulled. Perhaps a tiny sputter, nothing more. Already John had used four of his five pulls. So now he took the cord and wound it carefully around the flywheel. He checked all the settings, patted the motor on the side *and* the flywheel, and now he resorted to diplomacy. John talked to the Evinrude. He said, "Noo, for Moother, Gawd and Coontry." He said it with such feeling that I could fairly see the red and white, maple leaf flag of Canada snapping in the breeze to the tune of "Oh, Canada." John took the cord in his hand and pulled. And the Evinrude coughed, and sputtered, and roared to life!

Well, John had done it, got the motor going, as predicted, in 5 pulls. We settled down into our passenger seats, facing the stern or back of the boat so the wind would be at our backs. And John sat in the driver's seat so he could see where we were going. He threw the motor into forward, and soon we were speeding at full blast down the Kokechik toward camp.

Since we were sitting facing John we were forced to witness his smug smile, as he clenched his pipe in his grinning teeth, and his black beard blew in the wind, and he craned his neck to watch the river ahead with great satisfaction. But because we were facing the back of the boat we also were in position to see something else behind the boat. And so we saw, rising gradually from the depths and then skipping and spinning behind us on the surface of the Kokechik, our anchor, which we had forgotten after about my 30th pull.

So marvelous was the sight of our dancing anchor, following us on the end of its rope like a demented water skier, that we could do nothing but stare at it for several long seconds. John could see that our gaze was directed to the stern, and so he, too, turned and became fascinated by the sight of the dancing anchor. John thought to start slowing us down, but with him looking behind, no one was watching where we were going, and so he steered us right into the riverbank. The boat came to an abrupt stop. And the 40-horse Evinrude quit.

No one was hurt. And when we stopped laughing we took our one oar and pushed the boat out into the Kokechik as John prepared to make the first pull.

Part 2: The Circle of the Individual

Part 2: The Circle of the Individual

Although this part of the model (*Fig. 3*) refers primarily to the people for whom we are interpreting, in many ways it applies to us as well. We are not catalysts. When engaged in the interpretive process we are learning and growing as well as facilitating these processes in others.

The basic structure of this circle is not original. It reflects mandalas and shields from cultures around the world, which often include the same four facets of the human being: mental, emotional, physical, and spiritual. As much as possible, interpretation should address all these dimensions.

We are in the mental realm when we are focusing on cognitive aspects of interpretation: sharing facts and theory, seeking to facilitate understanding, designing program elements to accommodate analysis- and thinking-centered learning styles. Freeman Tilden's notion of "revelation" is directed mainly (though not exclusively) at this facet of ourselves.

The emotional realm swings our focus to affective aspects of interpretation: attending and attempting to influence attitudes; making use of Maslow's hierarchy of emotional needs; accommodating feelings-focused learning styles. Tilden's "provocation" appeals to our emotional side.

We are working in the physical realm when we are, for example, directing sensory and kinesthetic activities, which are the preferred learning styles for a good 3/8 of our constituents by some measures. It is the physical aspect of the resource with which we interact most directly, though that interaction has impacts that are mental, emotional and spiritual as well.

The spiritual realm has been under-represented in interpretive writing and training, I believe. Awareness techniques (Chapter 9) are an important entrance into this dimension, leading to the appreciation of beauty and, ultimately, love, the purest spiritual quality. I believe that when we are modeling behavior and attitudes, seed-planting, and dealing with intuitive learning styles (all topics to be dealt with in more detail later in this book), we are in the spiritual realm. Spirit intersects consciousness also through stories, via the dream-language of metaphor and allegory.

My motto is, "We are creatures made of stories, seeking to become creatures made of love." The circle of the individual revolves around this notion. Our daily lives are structured by our experience of cause and effect, the narrative, linear sequencing of events in time that accumulate as memories retained in a story format, with complex subplots and emotional colorings. Folk tales and myths place our personal stories in context and highlight their significance. Close metaphoric analysis reveals how these mythic stories, and by extension our lives, are packed with eternal values and qualities. I can think of none of these qualities greater than love; it is the common denominator in all the circles of the Deep Interpretation model.

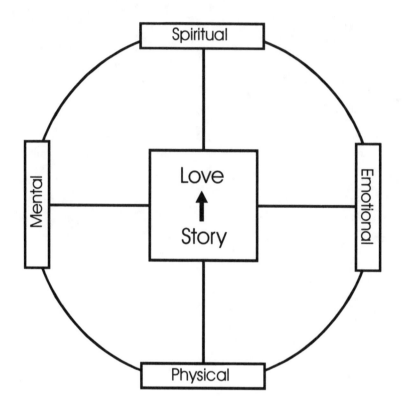

Figure 3: The Circle of the Individual

Chapter 5: Mind

Introduction to Learning Styles

Each of us has a unique way of thinking, perceiving, learning, and solving problems. Most adults appear to have limited flexibility in these matters. As a result, we often assume that everyone else should see the world as we do, and use the same approach in dealing with it. This is not true: each person's style has different strengths and weaknesses. Interpreters who understand this can be more effective, and in small ways can help people to develop their strengths and can promote tolerance of others' differences.

Every person has a unique personality, a product of both in-born influences and experience. Nevertheless, psychologists have found that there are clusters of personality characteristics which allow people to be placed in a few categories to ease understanding. Learning styles theories are intended to help educators deal with diversity in their students by assigning the many individual variations to a few categories. In practice such taxonomies work well, but we need to keep in mind that some people will not fit any given theory. I suggest, though, that as you read through the descriptions of the various systems below, guess which categories apply best to you, and see if you recognize acquaintances in the ones that don't.

The simplest systems, to give a somewhat familiar example, are the right brain-left brain systems. People who mainly use the left brain are best at logic, analysis, linear thinking, verbal conceptions, objective thinking, and a constellation of other things. People who mainly use their right brains are best at intuition, holistic thinking, visualization, subjective thinking, and imagining, among many others. Everyone balances the two to a degree, but the attractive simplicity of this scheme is lacking in reality---not that it's inaccurate, but we need to go beyond it to get to something usable. The other problem with the left brain-right brain model is that it's a dichotomy, and like many dichotomies it tempts people to choose sides, to determine which alternative is better.

Thinking Styles

I'll begin with C. West Churchman's system of thinking styles, as interpreted by Harrison and Bramson (1982). This set of 5 categories is limited to thinking and problem-solving strategies. Each is based on a different method of understanding the world and the nature of reality. A person is not in one category or another in this system, but rather is comfortable to different degrees with the different thinking styles. I can only briefly summarize these here, by listing some of the strengths each has in approaching problems. The system rewards a more in-depth study.

The most common thinking style is that of the Idealist, whose strategies include holistic thinking, taking a long-range view (seeing future impacts of current actions), setting goals and standards, receptive listening, identifying consensus and going from there, and humanizing the argument.

The Analyst thinking style is nearly as common as the Idealist. A person who is strong in this style can contribute a systematic analysis of alternatives, is willing to search for more data, is good at isolating variables one at a time when studying a problem, at charting the situation, at constructive nit-picking, and at deductive reasoning (drawing specifics from general principles).

The Realist, intermediate in frequency, sees a problem as something that needs to be fixed. Realists like to set hard objectives, keep in mind what resources are available, get to specifics, use expert opinion, simplify, and state corrections in no uncertain terms.

The Pragmatist is an uncommon style, but valuable when available. Pragmatists think in terms of moving one step at a time, experimenting and innovating (ready fire aim), looking for a quick payoff, tactical thinking, a marketing approach, and contingency planning.

The least common strategy is that of the Synthesist. Such a person operates by fostering open argument and confrontation, asking dumb-smart questions (superficially dumb, but with incisive depth that is not evident at first), suspending opposing ideas (entertaining them while waiting for an intuitive resolution or solution to emerge), making use of speculation and fantasy, proposing far-out solutions, and using negative analysis (what will go wrong if we do this?).

These different thinking strategies all have their strengths and their weaknesses. Different problems or situations call for different approaches. None is superior in any general sense. This helps us to comprehend the value of the more complex learning styles systems.

A Jungian System

The most venerable learning styles theory (Keirsey and Bates 1978, Myers 1993) has its roots in the work of Carl Jung and his followers. This approach defines four pairs of qualities that outline human character. Each of us expresses one of the qualities from each of these four pairs.

Introversion-Extraversion (abbreviated I and E, respectively) is the first choice: Introverts are oriented toward the inner world of thoughts and feelings. They draw energy from ideas, expend it in social situations, and recover it in solitude. Extraverts are focused on and draw energy from the outer world, are energized by people and depleted of energy when engaged in solitary activities. In the U.S., about 75 percent of the population are extraverts, 25 percent introverts.

A second pair of preferences is Sensation-Intuition (S,N). When gathering information, people with a sensation preference are focused externally, on sensory data, on facts (cf. the Realist thinking strategy). They believe in experience and history, and focus on the present, on concrete reality. Intuitives are focused internally on ideas, on the big picture, on the future, on metaphor, on imagination. They work with hunches (cf. the Idealist thinking strategy, above). Our population is about 75 percent S, 25 percent N.

The third pair is Thinking-Feeling (T,F), the former being more impersonal, analytical (cf. the Analyst thinking style), logical, rules-based and objective in decision making. People with an F preference are more subjective and emotional, with a more personal basis in decision making. Values are more important. Here the population distribution is close to 50-50, but there is a gender difference, with women more likely to be F's and men more likely to be T's.

The final pair is awkwardly named Judging-Perceiving (J,P). How do you orient toward the outer world? Are you more comfortable in the information-gathering stage (the S-N pair, above) or the decision-making stage (the T-F pair) of a process? "Judging" refers to individuals who are most comfortable with structure and who focus on closure and results. They have a work ethic, are serious, and are uneasy until a decision is made. "Perceiving" individuals take a looser, more playful approach and are more interested in process than product. They prefer to keep options open-ended and fluid, and resist making decisions. They have a play ethic, demanding that work process be enjoyable. Our population is about 50-50.

Children have not fully developed their choices, and are experimenting with all of Jung's preferences as they search for their own. This should be supported and encouraged---the choices are tendencies, and none are fully suppressed in a healthy adult. Diagnosing tendencies always is considered tentative in children .

An important lesson of this and other learning styles theories is that no learning style is more valuable than any other. Our society rewards the qualities of extraversion, sensation, thinking, and judging, in part because these are the more common, therefore familiar preferences, and in part because of sexual biases (women are more likely to be feelers, men thinkers). Our school systems reflect these biases, and a lot of people with less favored learning styles fall through the cracks unnecessarily. Educators who understand these concepts can be more responsive to the needs of their students.

Combining these preferences leads to sixteen possible combinations (ESTP, INFJ, etc.). This is an improvement over the unmanageable fact that every person's learning style is unique, but 16 variations still is an unwieldy prospect for the interpreter. The difficulty is resolved by combining preferences, usually in combinations of two letters. One system, that of temperament types

(Keirsey and Bates 1978), focuses on the combinations SP, SJ, NF and NT (each of the 16 types fits into 1 and only 1 of these 4 temperaments). The SP category, for instance, combines an externally focused, sensory orientation with a preference for process rather than product. Such a person learns best through action, sensation, and living in the moment (professional athletes, for example). An alternative way of combining preferences (Myers 1993), and one which perhaps is better from an interpreter's point of view, produces 4 communication styles:

- SP ("sensing"). People with this style emphasize concrete examples and practical information. They want brief responses, the bottom line, and like to get to the point. They like action, and prefer an emphasis on what is said and done rather than on the theory or thought behind it. Information is best presented step by step.

- NP ("intuitive"). Those with this style emphasize abstractions. Symbols and metaphors are important to them. They want the big picture, overview rather than detail. They enjoy creativity, variety, challenge, and are bored easily. They absorb information, like patterns and concepts, and read between the lines.

- TJ ("thinking"). These people are logical, analytical, critical. They are interested in principles, laws, organization, a formal approach, and detail. They cover the point thoroughly. They clarify by questioning, and want consistency and validity.

- FJ ("feeling"). A personal and human-oriented approach is preferred by people with this communication style. Human values, personal associations, trust and friendliness, and feelings are important. They want to be treated personally, like people and spontaneity.

You naturally will be inclined to communicate in your preferred style. Be alert for clues that you are not getting through. Knowing about these styles gives an idea of what to try if your first approach doesn't work. To find your style, first see how you orient to the outer world. If P, look at your information gathering preference (N or S). If J, look at your decision-making preference (T or F). Keirsey and Bates (1978) have a questionnaire that can identify your preferences.

An example of how I have taken advantage of this understanding is an experience in a classroom some years ago. A volunteer and I were presenting a program on raptors to a 4th grade class. The volunteer had taken out a live red-tailed hawk and was talking about it. After a short time, two boys got up and went to a table where we had placed feathers, wings, skulls and talons. They picked up a few items and returned to their seats to study them together. The teacher looked to me with a concerned facial expression, but I signaled to let it be. These boys had learned all they could from the passive viewing of the live raptor, and needed to handle and manipulate objects.

Learning Styles in Program Design

These combinations of preferences are enlightening, and four is a manageable number, but I found the concepts difficult to put into practice. They made me more sympathetic to the needs of individual kids, but how could I plan a program that would take these often conflicting needs into account?

That problem was resolved by Bernice McCarthy's (1987) 4MAT system. McCarthy has organized her learning styles categories into a logical sequence of instructional steps in lesson plan design. The steps expose each student equally to all learning styles. One of 4MAT's four learning styles, the analytic learners, corresponds very well to the thinking communication type. McCarthy's imaginative learners are closest to the feeling communication type. Her dynamic and common sense learners learners seem to correspond to the intuitive and sensing communication styles, respectively.

McCarthy further divides each 4MAT learning style in half, to accommodate the preferences different learners show for the left and right sides of the brain. Thus 4MAT lesson plans consist of eight steps and can take a considerable amount of time to complete, which is fine in McCarthy's original context of the classroom but difficult to achieve in an interpretive program. Thus, instead of McCarthy's eight tightly defined steps, I prefer four looser ones.

Nevertheless, McCarthy's sequence of learning styles makes a lot of sense, and I follow it. She begins with the imaginative (feeling) learners, whose need for self-actualization and preference for working in groups is met, typically, by a small-group activity which gives the students a concrete experience showing the relevance of the topic to be taught in the lesson. Next, she moves from that experience into a formulation of the concepts, a theoretical and analytical emphasis needed by people with the thinking communication style. In the third step, I replace McCarthy's common sense learning style with the intuitive communication type. The goal is to give the students an opportunity to play around with the concepts, as much as possible in personally chosen ways, so the students can make the concepts their own. In the final step, the closure-conscious sensory communicators are given satisfaction, preferably through the students teaching one another what they have learned.

Other Learning Styles Systems

So far I have outlined two systems of learning styles. Many others have been formulated. For example, a system being devised by Anthony F. Gregorc and interpreted in part by Butler (1987) shows promise of ultimately becoming the most comprehensive. At present its greatest strength, in my view, is the concept of bridging, a set of tactics for overcoming the difficulties students have when their learning styles conflict with the dominant one in a given lesson. I like such a particularized approach, and it can help during an interpretive program when a student is having trouble, but bridging does not play a role in program design.

An entirely different approach to learning styles is that of Rita Dunn and associates (e.g., Carbo et al. 1986). They list many factors (environmental, psychological, physical, etc.) that can affect a student's learning, and find for each student which ones are important. For instance, some students learn best in a quiet environment, others need noise, some want background music. Many of these factors are not considered in other learning styles systems, and are worthy of study by interpreters, but again the particularized approach limits the Dunn system's usefulness in program design.

Other Program Design Concepts

Learning styles represent only one category of theoretical approaches to education. A European system that is gaining followers in this country is SALT (Suggestive Accelerative Learning Techniques; e.g., Caskey 1980). SALT is designed for classrooms, but it has some features which I find appealing for interpretive programs. These include heavy use of guided imagery and other techniques that involve the subconscious; a pleasant, relaxed atmosphere; and a positive approach to learning that builds the student's self esteem.

Steve Van Matre (1990) also goes into the theoretical side of program planning. The many aspects of his Earth Education approach deserve a major place in interpretive programming. In particular, I am influenced by Van Matre's relentless focus on goals, his emphasis on helping the participants learn from their own experiences, and delightful elements such as "magic" and "hookers." On the other hand, a weakness of Earth Education is its neglect of some of the more passive learning styles. Earth Education programs seem designed especially for sensing communicators. This is not as bad as it might seem. Young children still are experimenting with learning styles, and most spend some time in each category while they are learning what works best for them. Thus, most children are capable of learning from Earth Education programs, though some are bound to be strained by them.

I also have benefited greatly from studying Native American teaching techniques. Particularization, assorted uses of storytelling (Caduto and Bruchac 1988), and the importance of community, connectedness and relationship are some of the elements of teaching in tradition-based societies that translate well into interpretive programming. The longitudinal nature of such traditional education (i.e., following the entire growth of each person and integrating him or her into a permanent, stable community with a shared spiritual orientation within an intimately known home landscape) limits its applicability in most interpretive situations.

Program Design Examples
I have just outlined a complex array of possibilities for program design, and my first suggestion would be that you review the original sources and put them together in your own way. I offer my own, four-step synthesis of these ideas as an example more than

as a model. I depart from the following framework myself when this seems necessary or appropriate. As I work my way through the plan, I will give examples from two of my programs, Tracking and Survival Human and Animal Style.

Step 1. Begin by giving the students a concrete experience that demonstrates the relevance of the study, makes it interesting, and preferably has social, group cohesion enhancing features. This part of the program focuses on the students who are feeling communicators, and can make use of ideas such as Earth Education's hookers, SALT's guided imagery, and particularization.

I begin the Tracking program by showing a photograph of footprints in the snow. I talk about how tracking is a language. I predict that the students will learn how to read a scene such as the one in the photograph. Then I break them into teams of five and give them sheets of paper with eight drawings of different mammals' footprints. I ask them to list four differences among the drawings. When they are done, we assemble and the teams take turns sharing their lists.

In the Survival program I break the group into teams of five and give them the following scenario. They are riding in a helicopter over a wilderness area. The helicopter fails, they crash land, no one is hurt but the helicopter explodes and they are stuck in the wilderness with nothing but the clothes they are wearing. There is no way of knowing when they will be rescued. They will have to see to their own survival until help comes along. Their assignment is to come up with a list of the things they need to acquire from the surrounding wilderness in order to survive. They also are to decide the order in which they need to obtain these things. They are not to worry, yet, about how they will obtain them. Again the teams report afterwards.

Step 2. Now we move from the initial experience to concepts, formulating the concepts in a clear and entertaining way. This is a necessary step for students with a thinking communication type. Some devices helpful here include guided imagery, storytelling, the use of slides or objects, and Earth Education's organizers.

In the Tracking program, I give the teams a second sheet of paper which lists the characteristics of tracks made by local mammal species. The mammals are divided into eight groups, one for each of the drawings on the first worksheet. I point out that the teams came up with all the characteristics on their own, and ask them now to use the listings on the second sheet to identify the drawings on the first. After they have done so, I demonstrate the four basic walking gaits used by mammals, and give the students an opportunity to try them out with me. I point out that each gait produces a distinctive pattern of footfalls.

The second step in the Survival program emphasizes the survival priorities of oxygen and shelter. Pointing out that we don't really need to do anything in a survival situation to obtain oxygen, I ask the children to take the time now to acknowledge where it comes from. I ask them to select a bit of lawn and to breathe on that grass, giving it some carbon dioxide, which it needs. Then they can suck out some of the oxygen it is producing in return.

Next the emphasis switches to shelter. In a wilderness we are surrounded by teachers. Our shelter-building teacher is the squirrel. I open a box containing a squirrel nest and ask the group to study it and identify its structural features. What ideas can we borrow in designing our own shelter?

Step 3. Now that the program's ideas have been presented, the time has come for the participants to try them out. The dynamic learners are action oriented, and the more physical and sensory the activity the better. At the same time, giving the students some choice is a good idea, so they can personalize their learning. Games and activities that give concrete form to abstract concepts, and practice in physical or mental skills, all fit here.

The Tracking program already entered this phase when the kids performed the gaits. We now move to an area where footprints are relatively easy to find, the muddy shores of a pond frequented by a variety of mammals. I allow the participants to move through the area as they wish, trying out what they have learned. Most are content simply to discover tracks and identify the species, while a few look at gaits, or follow the movements of an animal, or try to figure out what it was doing. I validate their discoveries and help with their questions.

The participants in the Survival program, having learned the design of a shelter, now build one scaled for my "assistant," a Cabbage Patch doll named Euell. After I critique their shelter by describing the kind of night Euell would experience in it, I move the students to the study of wild animal survival. They assemble their teams, and each team chooses a common wild animal of the area. I distribute cards that list the animals' source of food, water, and shelter, as well as the habitat where these things may be found. The teams go off to find examples of the habitats and search for the survival needs as well as representatives of their selected species.

Step 4. The final stage of a program can take different directions. Its focus is on the sensing communication type. This step should include an opportunity for students to teach students (for example, by sharing their own explorations from the previous step), and something from the interpreter to summarize or tie together the program. Earth Education's emphasis on applying the lesson to everyday life is important here. I sometimes include a carefully selected story in this step.

In the Tracking program, the students already have been sharing their tracking discoveries with one another. Now I take a step backwards in the design sequence, and introduce concepts of landscape tracking. In particular, I show how the structure of a tree tells the story not only of its own life, but of the landscape immediately around it.

Teams in the Survival program return from their exploration and report what they have found. I ask them not only about the species they studied, but also what other things of interest they found while wandering. I ask them to share with one another how they have obtained their survival needs that day.

Obviously this program planning scheme allows for considerable variation and creative expression on the part of the interpreter, but buried within all the detail is the most important idea. The ways in which we learn are as varied and as many as the number of individuals involved. All these variations deserve equal attention to the extent that we can give it. Honoring the differences in others may be the most important lesson of this study.

Defining Science

So much, for now, in the area of learning styles. Another area in which the mind of the individual takes a leading role is science. My own views as a scientist-in-training were shaped by philosopher Karl Popper (1968), who considered what he called criteria of demarcation in separating what is scientific from what is not. He pointed out that science is done by human beings, who cannot totally abandon their subjectivity. So science depends upon observations that are the same no matter who makes them. There is no way to prove that any hypothesis is true, because you can never be sure that an exception will not appear. But you can try to falsify a hypothesis, and if a hypothesis stands up to a variety of tests, it can be treated as though it describes a part of the physical universe correctly. Science is our best tool for understanding physical reality.

So far, so good. The picture is made fuzzy, of course, by the statistical nature of many phenomena in the natural world, as well as by chaotic determinism. The humanity of scientists leads them to bend the rules, often without being aware that they are doing so (Loehle 1987). These are points which have become better known in the years since Popper's treatise. But in my view they simply add interest and color to the basic structure outlined in the previous paragraph.

Of greater concern is the assertion by many scientists and others that science is, or should be, the only way to obtain knowledge. Extreme proponents of this view (e.g., Randi 1980) maintain that phenomena or aspects of reality that are inaccessible to scientific methodology simply do not exist. Popper pointed out that there are clear, logical limits to science and intrinsic uncertainties in its foundation. The whole range of metaphysical experience is subjective in nature and thus out of bounds to science. We celebrate this, in the arts and in religion. It is irrational to condemn such experiences in the name of science. They are not scientific, but that does not mean they are not real.

Uses of Science in Interpretation

I believe that our purpose as interpreters ultimately is spiritual in nature. There is nothing in science to contradict such a purpose, and I see nothing wrong with using tools such as science to support that good purpose. But we must be absolutely clear about ourselves and our tools, as well as our purpose. So let me go on now to talk about more concrete matters, the use of science's resources by interpreters.

Scientists rarely get involved in interpretation. But they do publish their results in the scientific journals. Even small college libraries subscribe to a variety of journals, and universities worthy of the name receive most of the important journals in the major academic areas. So interpreters don't need to go far or look very hard. I spend about 1-1/2 work days each year in reviewing about 15 journals, mostly in the areas of ecology and animal behavior. Among these I particularly recommend *Science, Ecology, American Midland Naturalist, Canadian Journal of Zoology,* and the *Quarterly Review of Biology. Natural History* magazine is a good popular source of sound scientific information.

During my library visit I look for papers of interest or utility to my interpretation---you would focus on different papers even if you chose the same journals. I skim titles, skim abstracts under interesting titles, and do spot reading in the texts of the papers themselves. I almost never read entire papers, unless they pertain to my own research interests. I trust the peer review process, although I recognize that mistakes can be made. I do use judgment, though: if my experience or the language of an author (too many qualifiers or hedging words) make me question a paper, I will make little use of its information. I also recognize theoretical papers for what they are, and am careful to qualify any references to them I may make in my interpretation.

I find that I frequently get ideas for new programs or ways to refresh existing ones from my study of the scientific literature. For example, studies of the reproductive ecology of Jack-in-the-pulpit (Bierzychudek 1982), which results in the death of the pollinating insects, added an interesting dimension to my spring wildflower walks. Showing my audience the dead flies inside the pulpits of female plants gave a positively artistic contrast to the sublime spring scene. The complexity of firefly display behavior (Lloyd 1980 and references cited therein) also has enriched the summers of many of my program participants.

A few years ago I got the idea to create dossiers for the different species of animals and plants, limiting the information in them to my own observations. I was embarrassed at how little I could write even for common species. The exercise prompted me to be much more conscientious in my observing and note-taking, and has resulted in a surprising jump in the vitality and credibility of my interpretation. The reasons for this, I suspect, include the fact that second-hand information I had "learned" from others or from books was not as vivid to me as were my own observations. Experience had taught me that the books and journals sometimes are misleading or wrong, so there were subconscious reservations about second-hand information I was transmitting. Also, I was accumulating a collection of stories from personal experience that made presentations more interesting. I recommend that interpreters try something like this dossier approach to the natural history stage of science.

And if you want to go whole hog, why not set up a scientific study of your own? You very quickly will learn how limited scientific methodology is. Your own interests will dictate the questions you will investigate. I find that the research forces me to notice things I might otherwise miss. For example, while measuring the phenology of leaves in forest plants I discovered that two species of spring wildflowers send up leaves in late autumn, thus extending their photosynthetic season with minimal risk of leaf loss to specialist insect herbivores. And again, your personal observations can't help but improve the vigor and freshness of your interpretation.

The history of the Earth, and the lives of the living beings that surround us, are a marvelous collection of fascinating stories. These were the basis of 10 years of columns I wrote for *Buffalo Bull*, the newsletter for Region 5 of the National Association for Interpretation. Here are a few of the stories from those columns, which ran under the collective name of "Scientific Sourcery."

Myrmecochory

The forest floor plants that flower and produce seeds in early spring have a problem. How will the trilliums, bloodroots, Dutchman's breeches, and others scatter and plant their seeds? In the fall, leisurely migrating thrushes and other birds spread seeds after eating the fruits of late-summer plants. Such birds are not as available when the spring plants reproduce: they migrate too early for some, too late for others. Probably they are in too much of a hurry to be reliable seed dispersers for any, since the birds that reach the breeding grounds first have the first choice of territories and mates. Also, the spring seeds are less attractive, lacking large size and not being contained in berries.

Ants that live on the forest floor also have a problem early in the year. Many ant species gather dead and disabled insects and other invertebrates for their food, but such foods do not become abundant until later in the spring or summer.

Through a gradually developing process of long-term interaction, many species of early plants and scavenging ants have helped to solve one another's problems. Myrmecochory is the dispersal and planting of seeds by ants. Botanists have long known that many early spring plants have unusual seeds, each with a ridge or flap that is conspicuous and pale in color. The flap, called an elaiosome, has evolved separately in several plant families. The elaiosomes of different kinds of ant-dispersed plants not only look alike, but also are similar chemically. They contain concentrations of fats which apparently resemble the ones in the invertebrate animals the ants eat. Further, the elaiosome provides a convenient handle the ant can use in transporting the seed back to the nest.

In the ant nest the elaiosome is eaten, but to the ants the seed is just an inedible residue. Seeds may be tossed into an underground waste chamber or simply left along a passageway, free to germinate. Early spring ants frequently move to new nest locations, so seeds are safe and may not accumulate in numbers that would lead to overcrowding after germination.

The significance of myrmecochory to the forest floor community in early spring becomes clear when we look at the proportions of myrmecochorous plants in a couple of forests. Ant-dispersed plants common in DuPage County, Illinois, forest preserves include wild ginger, large trillium, prairie trillium, bellwort, trout lily, Dutchman's breeches, bloodroot, many species of violets, and possibly spring beauty. In Meacham Grove Forest Preserve, 63 percent of the species and 80 percent of the individual plants that flower and fruit in early spring are ant-dispersed. Those same figures for Maple Grove Forest Preserve are 47 and 68 percent, respectively. Of course, the planting of seeds is not the entire story for these plants, since most of them also can multiply and spread through root growth. Without the ants to get them started, though, these plants would have a more difficult time. (This column was based mainly on a presentation at an ecology conference by A.J. Beattie and D.C. Culver).

Freshwater Jellyfish

(The first part of this piece I wrote as an Assistant Professor of Biology at a small college in Pennsylvania). Unfortunately, south central Pennsylvania does not have its version of the Loch Ness Monster, a large-scale biological mystery for a few of us to see and the rest to wonder about. Since we lack the mysterious, the best we can do is to seek the strange. My vote for the strangest local animal goes to a creature which inhabits lakes, like Nessie, but is much smaller than Scotland's much-sought "fearsome beastie." All I had heard about freshwater jellyfish before coming to Cumberland County was that they are rare, so I was startled one September day to see hundreds of the tiny, disk-shaped creatures cruising through the surface waters of Opossum Lake.

The Latin words *Craspedacusta sowerbyi*, when set in 12-point type, literally are larger than the body diameter of the animal they name. Bend those words into a circle and you have a closer idea of the jellyfish's size. The species was unknown until 1880, when it was discovered in a London botanical garden. That first individual apparently had been a stowaway in a shipment of water lilies from the Amazon River basin. Freshwater jellyfish now occur throughout Europe, and can be found in scattered ponds and lakes in the United States, mostly east of the Great Plains. No one knows whether the species is native to North America; the jellyfish stage of the life cycle appears most commonly in small man-made lakes and reservoirs, like Opossum Lake, and other stages are inconspicuous. Although it is more closely related to the dangerous Portuguese Man-of-War than to most of the typical jellyfish it resembles, the freshwater variety is harmless.

Craspedacusta starts its life as a tiny larva, swimming by means of numerous hairlike projections, called cilia, that work like little oars. The larva settles to the bottom of the lake and becomes a small, branching colony of tubes, or polyps, reaching a height of about one-third inch. The polyps feed by capturing small worms and other animals. Eventually the polyps produce buds which develop into young jellyfish, or medusae, that break off and swim away. The jellyfish capture small swimming animals, and by the end of the summer have grown to their full adult size; the two sexes of swimming jellyfish produce the ciliated larvae with which the life story began.

Opossum Lake's jellyfish were more difficult to find in 1980 than in the previous two years. I caught three in a bucket after finding a group of them in the middle of the lake. I kept the three in an aquarium, exchanging part of the water with new lake water each day, and two of the jellyfish lasted for more than two weeks. Little has been written about their interesting behavior. The jellyfish swim upwards, stretching their rim tentacles forward and converting their bodies into scoops that sift through the water. After reaching the surface they stop swimming and sink, still with tentacles outstretched, then right themselves and swim upward again. Most of their movement is vertical, although at times they swim horizontally for short distances.

I found myself watching the jellyfish more for pleasure than for satisfaction of scientific curiosity. These are beautiful creatures, and the two descriptions of them that satisfied me most emerged as a tune for recorder (a waltz, don't know why) and a bit of verse:

Blown-glass crystal, simple and free
Pulsing symmetrically:
Changing, timeless, moving, mindless,
Combing a freshwater sea.

Looking for jellyfish in Opossum Lake is much less expensive than a trip to Loch Ness, and more likely to produce the sighting of a genuine "beastie." (This column was based on Acker and Muscat 1976).

Postscript: Shortly after starting my new job with the Forest Preserve District of DuPage County, Illinois, someone spotted *Craspedacusta* swimming in one of the District's lakes, and District Headquarters called to ask if I knew anything about freshwater jellyfish...

Milk Sickness

The October of 1818 has touched the southern Indiana hills with brilliant colors. Tastes of crisp weather have beaten back the summer's humidity, but the brightness of the autumn sun is scarcely noticed by the preoccupied pioneer family. Inside the 18 x 18-foot, one-room log cabin, the young mother lies on the bed. She has been sick several days, and she knows from her nursing of similarly afflicted neighbors that she soon will die. The symptoms are clear enough: painful vomiting, constipation, reduced pulse and breathing rates, a horrible breath odor. The children, a girl of 11 and a boy of 9 years, wait on their mother. The father, when not busy constructing coffins for the neighbors his wife tended, does what he can for her. The end comes near and the mother, Nancy, calls Abe and Sarah, the children, to her side. Her last words to them are an admonition to love man and worship God. Soon afterward, Nancy Hanks Lincoln is dead.

Milk sickness must have been frightening to the pioneers, appearing at times and places difficult to predict. The ailment hit hardest in the central states of Illinois, Indiana and Ohio, as well as North Carolina, sometimes causing settlements to become nearly abandoned.

The exact cause of the disease was unknown for a long time, but it became associated in the minds of many pioneers with milk and milk products. Frequently the cows themselves suffered, showing some of the human symptoms but also a shaking, especially in the nose and leg muscles, that gave the disease the name "trembles."

Many hypotheses were created to explain "the milk-sick." Soil vapors, spider webs, bacteria, and the eating of poison ivy by cows all were blamed. After much debate and conflicting evidence had been tossed about the popular and scientific arenas, experimental studies in the early twentieth century finally demonstrated that milk sickness and trembles both were caused by the cows' consumption of white snakeroot (*Eupatorium rugosum*), a plant in the composite family. White snakeroot leaves and stems contain the poison, a complex alcohol named tremetol (after the Latin word for trembling), which may require the presence of other substances from white snakeroot tissues to produce its deadly effects. The alcohol dissolves readily in fats but not in water, so it concentrates in milk. Sometimes this removal is enough to delay or prevent damage to the cow.

White snakeroot grows in woodland clearings, apparently requiring a moderate amount of light. It is an annual, growing from seed through the spring and summer, and producing clusters of white flowers in the fall that are converted after fertilization to dandelion-like seeds.

White snakeroot normally is avoided by plant-eating animals, and often completely dominates a small forest opening. One of the more common herbivores of white snakeroot is a leaf miner, an insect so small that it fits between the upper and lower surfaces of the leaf, chewing its way through the center and leaving a network of tiny tunnels. Apparently the leaf miner is immune to tremetol, or perhaps the alcohol is concentrated in the leaf surfaces. Perhaps the presence of tremetol has provided a selective advantage to white snakeroot in its evolutionary struggle with herbivores.

Why is milk sickness not a problem today? There are at least two reasons. The first reason is that milk poisoning historically had a restricted distribution. Although white snakeroot grows practically throughout the eastern U.S. and adjacent parts of Canada, confirmed cases of the disease occurred only in a few states. Possibly tremetol or one of the substances with which it reacts is not present in most populations. Also, the current practice of mixing the milk of cows from a broad region should safely dilute any tremetol that a few cows could ingest. Livestock generally avoid white snakeroot when other forage is available.

The greatest danger of milk sickness today is to families who might drink their own cows' milk when the cows spend much time in woodlands containing the plant, or to careless natural foods enthusiasts who might be tempted to make a salad of whatever foliage is available. [This article was based on Kingsbury 1964, Muenscher 1975, and Warren 1959].

Fireflies

As I walked in the dark along a path through the forest, I noticed a faint, steady glow at the path's edge. I bent down and turned on my headlamp. In the sudden spotlight was a large firefly, but that insect had not produced the tiny spot of light. There was a small, half-eaten firefly dangling from the larger one's jaws. The dying glow of the victim had drawn my attention to the predator.

The many species of fireflies have several ways to avoid confusing one kind for another, so that their short lives are not spent chasing after unsuitable objects of insect romance. Some species live in separate habitats, others use timing to separate themselves, becoming active during different parts of the summer or at different times of night.

One final tactic identifies the few species that simultaneously use the same habitat. Each species flashes its own coded signal. The common lawn firefly, *Photinus pyralis* (no one has bestowed fireflies with standard English names), flies upward in an arc, sky-writing a line in the shape of a "J" or "U." A small firefly which commonly occurs where tall grass abuts forests in northeastern Illinois is *Photinus marginellus*, which emits a very brief single flash (a "dot" to *pyralis'* Morse-code-like "dash"). A third species which sometimes occurs with the others is *Photuris lucicrescens*. This one hovers motionless in one spot to flash, usually near a wet area with tall herbaceous plants. Its flash is prolonged and very bright, building in a crescendo-like fashion, hence the name.

Female fireflies, answering only their own males' calls with their own species-specific flashing reply, make the discrimination that allows love's true course to be followed. Or so it would be if the world were simple and boring.

Fireflies, it happens, are predators. From the moment they hatch from eggs laid on or near the ground, wingless firefly larvae scramble in voracious pursuit of soft-bodied creatures smaller than themselves. The predatory habit is retained in the adult, leading to one of the most bizarre facets of firefly biology.

Females of some of the large firefly species, including *Photuris lucicrescens*, spend much of their time after dark imitating the reply signals of females of smaller species like *Photinus marginellus*, in answer to the small males' flashes. The male, drawn by the wooing of a potential mate, becomes instead a meal. In some areas, individual predatory fireflies are known to answer and to prey upon as many as three different kinds of smaller fireflies.

This is the explanation of my observation in the forest. The larger firefly proved to be a female *lucicrescens*. Fortunately she left enough of the male that I could identify him as a *marginellus* (*Photinus* fireflies are identified by examination of tiny internal organs of the abdomen. I felt like an ancient soothsayer forecasting the future from a goat's guts).

If predatory female *lucicrescens* spend so much of their time calling hapless male *marginellus*, what do the male *lucicrescens* do? Certainly they spend part of their time performing the crescendo-like mating signal that gave their species its name, especially later in the night, but early in the evening, when *marginellus* males are busily emitting their tiny signals, they mainly imitate male *marginellus*. Why? The answer, suggests firefly ecologist James Lloyd, is that the males are pretending to be prey so that their own females will call them. The female, perhaps disappointed (can insects feel emotions? I know no way of proving one way or the other) by not calling in food, nevertheless may be persuaded by the presence of a male near at hand to continue with courtship and put off the search for dinner until later.

We are fortunate to have these creatures in eastern North America. People from west of the Rockies, where there are no fireflies, regard a yard full of fireflies with surprise and amazement. I do my best to follow their example. [The above account is based on Barber 1951, Green 1956, Lloyd 1965, Roeder 1963, and Williams 1917.]

"Knowledge"

I was doing my best to keep cool, but it wasn't working. The man was threatening to shoot me in the knees and vandalize my apartment. I defied him and he left, but I fretted over it. His girlfriend, who occupied the ground-floor apartment next door to mine, wanted me to remove the pan of water I put out for the birds, because a skunk was drinking from it in the evening and she didn't like having a skunk so close. "Knowing" skunks, I had argued for tolerance, confidently predicting that the animal would shift its activity to another part of its home range, as skunks typically do every few days. I had made that prediction over a month earlier, and the skunk was still coming.

My arrogance had come back to haunt me. I realized that the skunk's burrow must have been somewhere close. The best route for the skunk to take each night led past our apartments. Water was scarce that summer, and the skunk had found my bird-watering pan while digging grubs in the lawn in front of my patio. He may have varied his route in typical fashion, but only after getting farther along in his nightly wanderings.

I had forgotten one of my principles, that knowledge impedes learning. Now not only did I look stupid, which was deserved, but I had been threatened, and at the very least my neighbors seemed determined to kill the skunk if it kept coming. The drought had ended a couple weeks earlier, so I decided to withdraw the water. For the sake of my self-respect, or pride, I told the man what I thought of his tactics, and asked him to give the skunk a few days to establish a new routine. The skunk did shift his route so that it came no closer than 30 yards.

When you get good grades and are a "good boy" or "good girl," you build a self image as the fair-haired child who can do no wrong. Sooner or later you're in for a fall, and I had been tripping regularly in the months preceding the skunk incident. It was a time of eating ashes, to use Robert Bly's metaphor. Dragged kicking and screaming into my own mid-life crisis by my wife's, I found that the end of the marriage had not been the end of my humbling experiences.

Another confrontation came when a couple of elderly ladies challenged my delight in urban peregrines. They expressed their conviction that the local songbirds would be history after the falcons became established. I gave the standard assurances and explanations, but they would have none of it. There was proof, they claimed, in a scientific paper in *The Auk*, journal of the American Ornithologists' Union, the most prestigious North American ornithology publication. At the time there was little I could say. I hadn't seen that issue yet. I made peace as best I could while maintaining my position, and assured them that I would check their source.

Later I found the paper (Paine, Watton and Boersma 1990). Paine and company compared seabird populations before and after peregrines became established at an island off the Washington coast. Two species of petrels had shown no change, two auklets "are probably declining," but the falcons' consumption of northwestern crows or restriction of the crows' activities may have contributed to the observed increase in common murres, pelagic cormorants and black oystercatchers. "We conclude that the indirect, positive effects are at least as important to seabird abundance patterns as are direct, negative effects."

Thus the ladies' "knowledge" had resulted from a misinterpretation of the results. They were only seeking support for their pre-conceived notions, but the fact that they had gone to the scientific literature was to their credit. I had to laugh when I read a concluding comment by the authors: "In the long run, continually increasing peregrine falcons, a species that adjusts well to human activities and structures, will surely add a complicating and emotionally charged factor to the local conservation picture."

Wild Indigos

The wild indigos (*Baptisia* spp.) have spectacular flowers, large compound leaves with an attractive, bluish-green color, and enormous bloated seed pods. As I first got to know these prairie legumes I was struck by their strings of flowers, which run along the ground in some species, but stick straight up in others. I became intensely curious about why they should vary, but lacked the time to dig into the matter.

Then, while going through my routine literature review at a nearby college, I ran across a paper describing an investigation of that very question (Haddock and Chaplin 1982). The cream wild indigo (*Baptisia leucophaea*) and the white wild indigo (*B. leucantha*) flower at different times, and out of that single difference flows an array of consequences that gives the two closely related plants strikingly different personalities.

The first to flower is the cream wild indigo. Its large, lipped legume flowers require an insect pollinator with unusual strength to pry them open. In early spring there is one main candidate, the bumblebee queen. Only the queen survives the winter, and she must do all the work to get her colony going. She gathers food and tends the first brood of workers.

The problem for the cream wild indigo is that bumblebee queens are few and far between. There will not be many pollinator visits. Therefore, the plant is set up for self-fertilization. As in other wild indigos, the male flower parts are activated before the female parts, and the flowers along a string open in turn, beginning with the one closest to the center of the plant and moving outward. The cream wild indigo's strings of flowers are arrayed horizontally, so that the queen bee flying along the ground encounters the younger, male flowers toward the tip of the stalk first, then carries their pollen as she works her way inward to the female flowers. The costs of selfing are reduced genetic diversity and lower fertility, but there is a major advantage to this strategy, as we shall see.

The white wild indigo blooms much later, on average 45 days later at Haddock's and Chaplin's study area. By that time the bumblebee queens have produced enough workers that they can concentrate on laying eggs and running their nests, while the workers forage. Many more bees now are available to pollinate wild indigo flowers, and the plants can count on plenty of opportunities for cross-pollination. By displaying their flowers vertically, the plants not only make it easier for a worker bee to find them, but they also cause the bees coming in from low near the ground to visit the lower, older, female flowers first. Pollen from the previously visited plant is left on the female flowers, then the bee works its way up to the male ones near the top. The plant enjoys a very high seed set and, of course, the genetic advantages of outcrossing.

There is a catch, however. Because they wait until late spring or early summer, the white wild indigo plants are hit by much higher populations of seed predators, weevils and other insects that devour the developing seeds. By flowering much earlier, the cream wild indigos miss much of this seed predation, and as a result produce more seeds in an average year than does the white wild indigo, despite their lower seed set. In occasional years when predator numbers are low, white wild indigos come out ahead in a big way.

Earlier I used the word "personalities" in describing these plants. Given some money to invest, a cream wild indigo would go for conservative options, certificates of deposit and the like. It would have a smaller but more stable income. The white wild indigo would pack its bags for Vegas.

El Niño

Much has been written about *El Niño* and *La Niña* currents in the equatorial Pacific Ocean. An *El Niño* current is a short-term shift in oceanic currents which prevents a normal upwelling of deep, cold water from reaching the surface. The resultant warmer ocean surface can lead to higher temperatures or wetter precipitation patterns on continents some distance away through its influence on the atmosphere passing over it. The reverse of *El Niño* is *La Niña*, an unusually cold oceanic surface which can reduce precipitation and perhaps temperature in distant places.

A couple articles in 1990 addressed the ecological effects of such currents on terrestrial ecosystems. A paper by Thomas Swetnam and Julio Betancourt (1990) tied the alternation between *El Niño* and *La Niña* to patterns of precipitation and fire in Arizona and New Mexico. Swetnam and Betancourt showed that there is indeed a tendency for wet springs and small wildfires to be associated with *El Niño* and for dry springs and large wildfires to accompany *La Niña* episodes.

A more complex story arose in connection with an *El Niño* event in the Bering Sea (Zabel and Taggart 1989). *El Niño* currents, because they disrupt upwelling zones, cause problems for seabirds which depend upon the nutrient-rich deep waters to support abundant surface communities of marine organisms (i.e., dinner). In *El Niño* years, many seabirds choose not to breed. On the Round Island ecosystem studied by Zabel and Taggart, the eggs and young of seabirds are the major food of the red fox population. Normally the foxes are polygynous, with several females choosing to mate with those males whose territories contain large seabird nesting colonies. Such females lose the help of the male in raising their young, but gain access to an abundant, easily exploited food supply. But in *El Niño* years, the foxes switch to monogamy because each litter of pups requires two hunting parents.

I would like to share a personal note here. In 1975 I was finishing my Ph.D. thesis on the behavioral ecology of glaucous gulls in western Alaska. I was pointing toward a college teaching career, and decided to take a summer course in tropical ecology to balance my subarctic experience. We were hosted in Panama by the Smithsonian Tropical Research Institute. The course's lead instructor, Jim Karr, had worked closely with the Institute in his own research. Jim connected me with the Institute's director, Ira Rubinoff, who was looking for a postdoctoral student with experience in seabird research to pursue a study project for him. The study was to look at the potential effects of a then-little-known phenomenon called *El Niño* upon the colonies of boobies, pelicans and other seabirds off the Panama coast. It seemed like a sure thing, and the next step toward a high-powered university career. Rubinoff supported my application, and I more or less counted on it, but the parent Smithsonian Institution refused to support the project because it would take longer than a year. I ended up at a small college where the other faculty had a long history of hostility toward ecologists (I was among several others who lasted only a few years there), and that experience was so negative that I decided to change careers so here I am. The point of this anecdote is to demonstrate the bizarre ways in which ecological phenomena, even such apparently distant ones as *El Niño* currents, can have profound personal effects upon us.

Chapter 6: Emotion

"Besides, when you hit your thumb with an eight-pound hammer it's nice to be able to blaspheme. It takes a very special and strong-minded kind of atheist to jump up and down with their hand clasped under their other armpit and shout, 'Oh, random-fluctuations-in-the-space-time-continuum!' or 'Aaargh, primitive-and-outmoded-concept on a crutch!'" (Terry Pratchett 1993, *Men at Arms* [novel]).

Blending the Affective and Cognitive

A few years ago, during the van drive home from the National Association for Interpretation's Cleveland Workshop, several of us DuPage County interpreters got into a conversation about the affective and cognitive dimensions of interpretation. I don't remember much about the details, but it seems to me we all were assuming an either-or model for the process, and making our various arguments about whether we should begin with information and proceed to feeling, or go for the gusto first and fill in the facts later. Emerging understanding from brain researchers is telling us that these two aspects of learning may not be as separate from one another as educators have believed. The first part of this chapter is based on two recent books (Damasio 1994 and Goleman 1995), both of which should be readily accessible through local libraries.

We've long known that information flows into the brain from assorted sensory inputs that provide images of the body and of the surrounding world. What is new is the discovery that the information is split, simultaneously going to more than one part of the brain for different forms of concurrent processing. One set of incoming signals goes directly to the amygdala, which are structures within the relatively ancient limbic system, an outgrowth of the brainstem. Another, more complete set of the sensory information goes to the cerebral cortex. The cerebrum carefully and more slowly analyzes and interprets the images coming to it, making sense of them and thinking about them. This takes time, and thus does not produce our first response. That comes from the amygdala, which store a vast number of remembered images (visual, auditory, etc.) from past experience and very quickly compare the new signals to this library.

The amygdala are not simply seeking the familiar. They are our primary storehouses of basic emotional associations. They can set off rapid bodily responses, driven by emotion, either of avoidance or attraction (I remember, as a child in a family notorious for its fear of spiders, turning over a board on the ground and suddenly finding myself 50 feet away from that spot, registering in consciousness the large wolf spider that had been under the board). The amygdala also can simply give impressions of like or dislike for what is being perceived (is my dislike of the color pink connected to the foul-tasting pink medicines, and the associated unpleasant feelings of illness, I experienced as a youngster?). These responses and impressions often are established when we are very young, and before we have the ability to form much of a conscious memory of the foundational experiences. This makes it difficult for us to override the responses consciously, though with experience we develop a more sophisticated variety of emotional associations in the prefrontal lobes of the cerebral cortex (as an adult I forced myself to study the anatomy of spiders under the microscope, largely reducing but by no means eliminating my reaction to them).

One upshot of all this is that we respond with both analysis and emotion to incoming stimuli. Attempts neatly to divide the cognitive and affective realms in education therefore are doomed to fail. As interpreters we take advantage of this when we attempt to make our offerings exciting, fun and interesting. The information we pass on thus becomes associated with a positive emotional tag or aura. The same beneficial feeling is tied to our facilities and to us as guides.

Goleman describes studies suggesting that in learning situations, a new skill or concept needs to challenge one's ability slightly if optimal learning is to take place. We interpreters will succeed best when we set up enjoyable experiences that strike a balance between boredom, on the one hand, and anxiety about performance on the other. This is why we need to pay careful attention to the developmental level of our audience and seek to balance our programs' appeal to the range of learning styles.

One important theme common to the two books is that people with damaged emotional circuits make bad decisions. Even if all the logical and informational centers of the brain are untouched, the inability to access emotional associations, necessary for judging good or bad implications of possible choices, results in disastrous lives for those so afflicted. Logic alone, Mr. Spock, is insufficient. The classic example, with which Damasio opens his book, is the case of Phineas P. Gage. Gage was a railroad construction worker in the 1800's, popular and personable, with a promising career ahead of him. This ended when a freak accident blew a tamping rod up through his chin and cleanly through his forebrain. The pointed, 1-inch-thick missile later was found some distance away. Its bullet-fast flight had not killed Gage, as one might expect. Within minutes he was conversing with co-workers. Before many days had passed, however, it became clear that his judgement was destroyed. He had acquired antisocial mannerisms and lost his work discipline. The prefrontal lobes, so critical for modulating and controlling his emotional response to stimuli and events, had been damaged beyond repair.

Goleman's definition of "emotional intelligence" is worth remembering. He gives many examples of studies showing that IQ is less of an indicator of success (now matter how you define success) than is emotional intelligence, displayed best by people "who know and manage their own feelings well, and who read and deal effectively with other peoples' feelings" (p. 36). Components of emotional intelligence include optimism; the ability to manage anger, fear and worry; "flow" (closely related to what I have referred to as "seeing purely" in awareness studies); and intuition.

Damasio proposes a fascinating hypothesis for how gut feeling (a form of intuition) works. He believes that parts of the brain storing emotional memories recognize patterns in the current situation, and send out signals causing the body to produce what we sense as negative or positive gut feelings. These steer us away from or toward certain courses of action.

Damasio also looks into implications of brain studies on what the mind is and how it works. His starting point is that the mind depends upon a particular capacity: "the ability to display images internally and to order those images in a process called thought" (p. 89). Damasio argues that there is no single brain site where everything comes together. Our sense of a single conscious focus or subjective point of view is "a trick of timing," with the co-occurrence of activity in several brain regions giving the illusion of being one process.

Damasio would like to avoid the stigma of reductionism. In the end, though, he makes as strong a reductionistic, deterministic statement as I have ever seen. I must admit, he makes sensible hypotheses about how the brain creates the sense of self (an "endless reactivation of updated images about our... past and...the planned future"), and subjectivity (a postulated network examines the self, along with new environmental or bodily stimuli, and registers the resultant changes in the self).

Nevertheless, Damasio's rejection of a nonphysical soul, or spirit, is premature. Like so many scientists, Damasio fails to understand the mythic foundation of science, as discussed in the last chapter. He could be completely right, as far as he carries the physical-biological processes he studies, and yet still not be telling the whole story. In terms of logic, Damasio confuses necessary conditions with sufficient conditions. Damasio is a physician who deals with damaged brains. He finds, not surprisingly, that a damaged brain limits the range of behavior and understanding of the person possessing it. But the fact that an intact brain is a necessary condition for mind's full expression in the physical world does not mean that other necessary conditions could not exist. In spite of these mistakes, the fascinating work that Damasio and other students of the central nervous system are doing has much to offer interpreters and other educators, and I for one will be following their further progress with interest.

Maslow's Hierarchy

A concept I have found useful in the understanding of emotion is Maslow's hierarchy, which can be briefly described by the phrase "first you pee, then you see." (Nancy Fischer, as quoted by Barbara J. Stewart in 1992 NAI National Workshop Proceedings)

For most of us, Maslow's hierarchy (e.g., Maslow 1970, chapter 5) is one of those boring theories of doubtful relevance we run into when studying introductory psychology, expecting never to think of it again. But Maslow's model remains the best description of human emotional needs we have. Thus, affective realm interpretation and particularly the understanding of attitudes, their development and what is needed to change them, requires a study of Maslow's ideas. After all, an attitude is (Webster's Third New International Dictionary) "a disposition that is primarily grounded in ... emotion ... a persistent disposition to act either positively or negatively toward a person, group, object, situation, or value."

Before Abraham Maslow came along, psychologists had listed and categorized emotional needs. What he added was a cohesive framework. Maslow proposed that these needs are arranged in a particular order. Basic needs must be satisfied before a person is ready to attend to more refined ones (thus Fischer's quote). This is relevant to attitudes because attitudes often are influenced by whether their object blocks or facilitates the meeting of some need.

For instance, people oppose crime because it threatens safety.

What led me into this topic was the need to get a handle on peoples' attitudes toward wildlife. I work at a wildlife center, where we specialize in educating people about wildlife and in performing wildlife rehabilitation. Our mission is "to champion harmonious coexistence between the people and wildlife of DuPage County and to promote diverse and healthy wildlife populations." The thousands of telephone calls we get each year tell us that a lot of people are not ready to consider harmonious coexistence with wildlife. Many belong to the the-only-good-raccoon-is-a-dead- raccoon school of wildlife relations. I found that Maslow's theory gave me a good understanding of what we observe in our constituents.

According to Maslow, the most fundamental needs are physiological (hunger, thirst, etc.). A child who really really needs to go to the bathroom is not going to place a very high priority at that moment on learning about habitat. With regard to my suburban county, this category of needs is not particularly relevant to attitudes toward wildlife because the principal physiological need wild animals could meet would be as the Main Course. In a more rural community where hunting and fishing are part of the culture for a significant segment of the population, physiological needs would have to be included in the mix.

The next level in Maslow's hierarchy is safety and security needs. This one is extremely important, and not just in attitudes toward wildlife. Advertising, notably promos for TV news programs, relies heavily on peoples' fundamental concern for safety and security. "Some of the large trucks on our highways don't have good brakes. Watch our news program at 10 and find out more." This kind of advertising blatantly exploits peoples' fears. It also reflects the ad writer's mastery of Maslow. At the Willowbrook Wildlife Center we see that many people are afraid of wild animals, and that the bulk of this fear is ungrounded or misinformed. Until we reassure and educate people out of their fear, they are not going to be receptive toward our messages about the benefits of positive human-wildlife relationships. Out of my study of this subject I wrote a series of 36 "attitude statements," notions about wildlife that we wish to promote in our constituents, arranged in the order of Maslow's hierarchy. An example of one of those addressed to safety and security needs is number 4: "Animals seek to meet their own survival needs, not consciously to cause fear or inconvenience to people."

The next emotional need is for belongingness and love. This basic need underlines the importance of treating our visitors with respect, even when they disagree with us. To the extent that we can relieve peoples' fears of wildlife, we may open them to attitude statements such as number 11: "Wild animals belong in suburban neighborhoods, and efforts to exclude them are impractical."

The need for esteem, for the achievement and gaining of recognition, is tied, I think, to peoples' humane concerns for wildlife. We hold in high regard those who treat people and animals humanely. The Jeffrey Dahmer case brought out that mass murderers typically tortured animals when they were children. Thus this is not a trivial matter, and even a humble nature center can promote values of general social benefit. Of the many attitude statements addressed to this emotional need, numbers 14 and 15 address this point directly: "14. People who treat animals humanely tend to treat people and property well. 15. The converse of (14) also is true: people who intentionally or neglectfully mistreat animals tend to mistreat people and property, as well."

We now reach the place in Maslow's hierarchy where a person, having satisfied more elemental emotional needs, is ready to meet his or her cognitive needs, for knowledge and understanding.

At this point natural history information becomes interesting in and of itself. A person then is open to the possibility that wild animals might be enjoyable to learn about. Statement number 31: "Wild animals and plants can be profound teachers."

Close on the heels of cognitive needs are aesthetic needs, for order and beauty. Number 32: "Wild animals, plants and other wild components of the landscape are beautiful." A person who has reached this point is receptive to notions that the beauty of nature is a value worth preserving for its own sake.

The pinnacle of Maslow's hierarchy is the emotional need for self-actualization (realization of potential). This part of his model is somewhat controversial. Is self-actualization truly a peak for everyone, or only for some? There is also the fact that the concept of self-actualization is vague and open to interpretation.

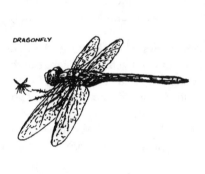

DRAGONFLY

Maslow (1970, chapter 11) lists qualities of people he regards as self-actualizing. Some of these qualities are acceptance, spontaneity, the ability to be comfortable with solitude, peak experiences, human kinship, humility, respect, deeper and more profound human relationships, ethical clarity, creativity, resistance to enculturation, and the ability to resolve, absorb or unify dichotomies. Given the difficulty this concept poses, my only stab at a related attitude statement to date is no. 36: "Willowbrook offers volunteer opportunities for those who wish to help in public education or animal keeping."

My own view is that spiritual matters, and especially love, sum up much of self-actualization as Maslow seems to be defining it. Accordingly, the centers of the three circles of my interpretation model are connected to Maslow's hierarchy. In the circle of the community, we begin in survival mode (interdependence) but progress to love. Similarly, the circle of the interpreter moves from technique to love and the circle of the individual moves from story to love. Speaking of stories, as you read the following one, please don't make the mistake of assuming it is about eagles.

Bill and Stella

Stella was a big, beautiful female Golden Eagle from the Caucasus Mountains in what was then the Soviet Union. Bill was a slim, trim, male Golden Eagle from Montana. They met in a cage at the Brookfield Zoo near Chicago.

Stella was the first to speak: "Vhat hoppened to you?" She admired Bill's profile as she tried not to stare at the empty space on his left side.

"Shot," Bill said. "Rancher shot me. Thought I was going to fly off with one of his steers or children or somethin'. They couldn't do anything for the wing, so they cut it off. You can call me Hop-along Bill."

"Vell, Hops-along, I like Bill. Is good name, Da. Stella, dot's my name, Aquilavitch. I vass diving down on a hare in the Caucuses. Broke wing on telegraph wire. Can fly, now, but only liddle bit."

"I don't know if an American Golden Eagle, and a right winger at that, oughta be hangin' out with a Russian. But they put us together so it must be okay. You're a good looker, Stell."

The years went by, and Brookfield Zoo grew. The two golden eagles were occupying space that was needed for more exotic animals. They were moved to the Willowbrook Wildlife Center, a wildlife rehabilitation center in nearby Glen Ellyn. The eagles seemed to like it there.

"Now, Stell, this is more like it. Quiet, not too many people, nice big cage...plenty of space for you to spread your wings."

"Da, but...is big shame you can't fly, too, Aquilavitch."

"Yeah, it twists my tail feathers all right. But mainly because I cain't court you proper, Stell. Why, I can just see the two of us a mile high in the sky, doin' loop the loops and pinwheels, then divin' straight down together...Some day, Stell, some day it will happen. There will be some way for us to do that courtship flight."

"If anyone can find a vay, you can, Aquilavitch."

The two golden eagles became one of Willowbrook's most popular exhibits. For years, people would come, and they would ask the first staff member or volunteer they saw, "Do you still have the eagles? Where are they?" And we would point them toward the biggest cage at Willowbrook. Yes, those eagles were special, all right.

"Hey, Stell, look at this. The animal keepers down there. They're picking up those feathers we dropped last night. What do you think they're doin' that for?"

"Who knows? Crazy capitalist American humans. Maybe they vill make you new wing, Aquilavitch, so ve can have our courtship flight."

Native Americans from around the Chicago area often stopped by just to see the eagles. Sometimes they asked pointed questions of the staff: "Are you taking good care of those eagles? They're special to us, you know." We didn't mind the questions because we knew we were taking good care of the birds. In fact, we picked up the eagles' feathers when they molted them and we sent them on to the federal government for distribution to Native

GOLDEN
EAGLE

Americans who needed them for traditional clothing and ceremonies. They, might, for instance, make a pair of wings to wear and then perform a dance based on the golden eagles' courtship flight.

The eagles were caged, and you could easily get the impression that they were separated from the surrounding ecosystem, but now and then they would demonstrate the foolishness of that notion when an opossum would smell the eagles' food and squeeze through the bars for a snack. Stella would come swooping down, and instead of enjoying a happy-meal the opossum became one instead. Stella may have been the only golden eagle who hunted successfully on her own in both the U.S.S.R. and the U.S.

Every spring Stella carried sticks in her talons or beak up to the top of one of the artificial trees in the cage and built a nest. And then one spring something special happened.

"Come and see, Aquilavitch. Come and see."

"All right, I'm comin', it just takes a while to hop up there. Now what's all the excitement abou...Why. It's a egg!" There was a moment of silence, then, "All right, Stella, whose egg is this?"

"It is mine, Aquilavitch. Mine alone. It von't hatch. No courtship flight, remember?"

Eventually the eagles became more than thirty years old. The eggs stopped coming, and there was less and less nest-building each year.

One day the male, Bill, died. We all watched Stella for signs of mourning, but eagles don't have facial expressions. She continued to save him a spot on the perch as though he were still there, but that was all we could see. Then, a week later on a sunny April day, Stella passed away. That was a strange day. The cage was quiet and empty. But high in the sky overhead, if you looked out of the corner of your eye rather than straight at it, you could see a strange sight. There were two faint shadows, each with two broad wings, doing triple loop-the-loops and then diving, pinwheeling, falling...together, forever and ever, through a bright, blue, warm April day.

Chapter 7: Body

In winter I help teach kayaking at one of several courses offered at swimming pools around the Chicago area by the Chicago Whitewater Association. Most of us who help teach are one-on-one instructors in the Eskimo roll. This was my first experience in teaching complicated physical movement, and at first I found it very different from other teaching and interpreting I had done. But before long, reflecting on my own experiences when learning to roll, and applying some interpretive techniques, I was able to get a handle on the process and gain some confidence.

The Eskimo roll is a complex sequence of motions performed through three dimensions, by a person who is upside down and under water with the lower half of the body confined in a small boat. The student's brain is quick to point out that this is an entirely new thing to be doing, and most people find it at least a little scary at first. The very first thing we teach new people in the water is how to get out of their boats when upside down. The second thing we teach is that, if they signal us, we can turn them upright very easily. With these two forms of escape established, we can begin to teach the various parts and aspects of the roll.

A standardized sequence of instruction in the Eskimo roll has been developed which works for most kayak students most of the time. Yet we see that every student is different. Some take to the standard technique readily, others have difficulty from the start, most get hung up at some point. This is never a time for blaming either oneself or the student. Often, perhaps usually, it has something to do with conflicting learning and teaching styles.

The first relevant factor to review in learning styles is that some people are introverts (I), others are extraverts (E). Extraverts are energized by other people. Introverts are energized by ideas.

Extraverts lose energy when they are alone. Introverts lose energy in crowds. Neither is good or bad, better or worse than the other. Introversion-extraversion is not a description of two learning styles. It is a factor which contributes to them, however. My own observation is that sea kayakers are more likely to be introverts, whitewater paddlers extraverts.

Another factor is sensing (S) versus intuition (N), which I think is very important in kayaking. People with a sensing bias are externally focused, while those with an intuitive bias are more inwardly focused, toward either thoughts (T) or feelings (F). Three quarters of the general population are sensing, or externally focused. That proportion probably is inflated among whitewater paddlers. Thus many instructors run into problems when dealing with intuitive students (as an intuitive-biased instructor, I am able to help other intuitives with relative ease). The T-F factor is the only one with a gender difference. Men tend to be more thinking oriented, women more feeling oriented, but this is not hard and fast.

And not all sensing people are the same, either. Some are more accomplishment focused (J), others are more focused on process (P). A process-focused student will be more likely to be satisfied with week to week progress and the physical activity of paddling, trying things out, and learning. An accomplishment focused student is more likely to point toward the end result and be less satisfied with anything short of perfection, or at least of having learned something.

As children we are more or less balanced in all these areas. All of us hang onto little pieces of all these temperament types within us. When we are doing whitewater kayaking, loving that moment to moment excitement, we are touching base with the action freak part of us. When we look back on a day's paddle with satisfaction, we are living within the accomplishment part of us. And when we reflect upon what kayaking means to us, either the feelings or thoughts it gives us, we are participating in the internally focused part of ourselves.

We tend to teach in a style that reflects our own learning style or temperament type. We will be most helpful to students who share our individual styles. When we are having trouble teaching a student, we should not feel bad, about ourselves or about the student. All learning styles are equally good. But a mismatch, if never addressed, can lead to frustration. How can we minimize the problems?

One way that works for us in these pool classes is to encourage students to work with many different instructors, unless there is rapid progress in a student-teacher team right off the bat. In that case that team should be kept together as long as progress continues to be rapid or until the student has the basic idea. If we understand our own styles, we can be on the alert for particular students we may be able to help. I am internally focused. My breakthroughs in the roll came when certain instructors explained the process in ways I could visualize. I made slow progress with instructors whose style was to concentrate on all the little movements that make up a roll, moving my body through the correct positions without giving them a context or tying them together. Only after I was helped to find the correct visualization, something to which I could hook those movements, did it make any sense. The standard techniques of teaching the roll work well for most students, but we need to be on the alert for clues, and to be prepared to address mismatches by accommodating to the student's learning style or recruiting other instructors we think may be better matched.

Instructors seldom think about or address the physical intimacy involved in teaching the roll. We should, because there is a lot of it, and to internally focused students, especially introverted ones, this aspect of the class comes as a surprise and may lead to discomfort. It is necessary that we balance and support the students' bodies when needed, and we need sometimes to move them correctly through a sequence of actions. We need to acknowledge the potential discomfort, and explain why it is necessary.

Internally focused, feeling oriented students (NF's: 12 percent of the general population) will consider the personal interaction with the instructor to be very important, and may want to work with the same instructor week after week. This is good, and such a student may progress best if not jumping from one instructor to another, but only if there is a good instructor-student match in learning and teaching styles. I find that internally focused students benefit from being encouraged to work on visualizing aspects of what they are learning during the week between classes.

Internally focused, thinking oriented students (NT's: 12 percent of the general population) will not progress unless things are explained to them. Doing the movements is not enough, and will lead to frustration. In such a person, the *idea* of kayaking is more important than actually paddling, at least at first. I mentioned this point at a workshop for kayak instructors, and it was fascinating to see how a majority were surprised and disbelieving, and a small minority were smiling and nodding with self-recognition.

Externally focused, action oriented students (SP's: 38 percent of the general population) probably will progress most quickly with our standard sequence of instruction, and almost certainly are disproportionately drawn to whitewater kayaking in the first place. The discipline of repeated practice may be boring to them, however, and they need to be urged to do things over and over. While their tendency to want to always be trying something new and experimenting is good, sometimes it can get in the way.

Externally focused, results oriented students (SJ's: 38 percent of the general population) can best be helped by focusing on the little, successful steps they make each week. Sure, they may not have a complete roll, but they are, for example, doing a good job of getting the paddle out of the water in setting up. I like to emphasize those small successes and give them something to build on.

The interpretive method of analogy to common experience is very useful in teaching the roll. For example, one common problem is a student's tendency to lift the head too soon (making the rising boat top-heavy and overbalanced before it is fully upright, causing the paddler to fall back under the water). I use the analogy of pouring beer into a glass. The kayak is the glass, and you first snap your hips and legs to turn it upright. Then you pour yourself into your vessel, your fluid body filling it from the bottom up, and topping it off with a head. Other instructors have a shorter, pithier mnemonic: butt-head.

It's an intensive, creative form of teaching. Students always are amazed at the instructors' patience, but we all remember the obstacles we met and the problems (ultimately recognized as self imposed) we had to overcome. It is, for most students, so much more than simple physical movement. It's an emotional, a conceptual, sometimes even a spiritual journey. Several hours of one-on-one instruction often are required before a student's first, often somewhat wobbly, roll, and huge cheers from all the instructors immediately reward and acknowledge that success.

The following little story (traditional, from the Okanagan, Teit et al. 1917) and poem (my own creation) both refer to the body. The latter also is about recycling.

Old One (Okanagan)

Old One, or Chief, made the Earth out of a woman and said she would be the mother of all the people. Thus the Earth was once a human being, and she is alive yet, but she has been transformed and we cannot see her in the same way we can see a person. Nevertheless, she has legs, arms, head, heart, flesh, bones and blood. The soil is her flesh, the trees and vegetation her hair, the rocks her bones, and the wind is her breath. She lies spread out, and we live on her. She shivers and contracts when cold, and expands and perspires when hot. When she moves, we have an earthquake.

Old One, after transforming her, took some of her flesh and rolled it into balls, as people do with mud or clay. These he transformed into the beings of the ancient world, who were people, and yet at the same time, animals. They were the ancestors of the people and animals we know today. Thus, everything living sprang from the Earth, and when we look around we see everywhere the parts of our Mother.

Blood Hands Crossing

I.

At All Spirits Port, near Blood Hands Crossing,
They meet for the first and final time.
Trees quaff ale, as men suck soil
In an open exchange of viewpoints.
You can take a turn to talk to a rock or Socrates,
And the ghost ships come and go with the tides.

I watch them, sometimes, the captains with their
      empty eyes,
The ships with sails pale and tattered,
And wonder if I dare seek passage.
But my brother waits at Blood Hands Crossing,
His dead voice draws me back,
And I will go to him soon.

II.

At Blood Hands Crossing, near All Spirits Port,
I waited, the black wind whistling between my ribs.
A low-crowned hat sat on my head.
Its jaunty plume puffed scarlet.
I seized the sword in my skeletal hand
As though I knew he would come,
But one word only echoed through my empty skull:
      Revenge,
Revenge for a dagger in the back.
The fat moon was naked but for a wisp of dark cloud
That reflected obscenely in the puddled ruts
Of Blood Hands Crossing.

He came then, my brother, and stood before me.
Fool! He turned his back and waited, weaponless.
I grinned and ran him through.
But as he fell his flesh dissolved,
The spell reversed,
My meat returned!
And, whole again, I completed my nakedness,
And tossed the hat upon his head,
And placed the sword in his skeletal hand,
And---for a time---left him there
At Blood Hands Crossing, near All Spirits Port.

Chapter 8: Spirit

"The finest uses of national parks, or indeed of any of the preserves that come within the range of interpretive work, lie ultimately in spiritual uplift. This end cannot be reached except through a walk with beauty of some aspect, in which the interpreter is not primarily a teacher, but a companion in the adventure." (Tilden 1977, end of chapter 11)

Defining Spirit

When I conceived the general notion of Deep Interpretation, I felt that the topic of spirituality would be a major theme. After all, I had stated several years earlier (Strang 1989b) that "Nature interpretation is teaching people to hear and understand the languages of the Earth. But an interpretive naturalist is a healer---someone who lovingly salves and binds the conceptual and spiritual wounds separating people from their Earth Mother." Certainly there is evidence that many in our society are searching for spiritual meaning. Churches are filling, the New Age subculture has influenced the general culture in many ways and drawn people alienated by traditional religion, popular songs increasingly treat religious topics, and films with spiritual themes (*Forrest Gump, The Shawshank Redemption*, etc.) have had great success. Practically every popular, general talk about "nature" and its significance that I hear makes reference to the wilds as a spiritual treasurehouse.

But like many or most interpreters, I work for a governmental agency where church and state separation is an institutionalized (even Constitutionalized) value. Because of that, and because I don't feel compelled to burden you with every detail of my personal beliefs, the question becomes, can we separate spirituality from religion, and legitimately focus on the former in our interpretive work? That interpreters as a whole are split on such issues was revealed in Matt Zuefle's (1994) Ph.D. thesis study of interpreters' religious values and environmental ethics. When asked whether "religious issues are appropriate for discussion in interpretive programming at public agencies," 40% of those polled said "yes," 34% said "no." A higher plurality of 47% agreed (vs. 24% who disagreed) that "interpretation can effectively be mixed with spiritualism or mysticism."

I believe we can focus on spirituality, thus skirting religion altogether, but the distinction leads to a peculiar limitation. Religion is specific and definite, consisting of the myths, ceremonial practices, and particular beliefs with which a group of people approaches spiritual mysteries. Spirituality is generalized and indefinite. Yet the more one talks about spirituality, the more specific and definite it seems to become. Thus, less space will go to this topic than I once expected.

As an interpreter I see two approaches we can take to spirituality as separate from religion. One approach is to look for a common denominator among all religions, and focus on that. For example, Joseph Campbell (1968, 1988) has shown how there are common themes or elements to the mythic foundations of most if not all religions. But this approach has the problem that atheists (those who reject all religion) might object, which would put government-employed interpreters in the position of possibly alienating or unintentionally mistreating some of our constituents.

The other approach is to look for aspects of spirituality which are common to human experience, shared by atheists and people of all religions. This approach demands a definition of what spirituality is in the first place. I will draw on the work of two scholars in particular: a British researcher named Sir Alister Hardy, and someone whose ideas already have appeared in an earlier context, Abraham Maslow.

I define *spirit* as an aspect of reality regarded as being incapable of perception through the physical senses in any objective way. It is experienced subjectively, through emotions or feelings, visualizations, artistic inspirations, peak experiences (epiphanies), etc. Notes: spirit often is thought to underlie and perhaps permeate the physical universe, to be connected to it but not dependent upon it (though the reverse may be true), and to be more essential, more important, or more permanent or eternal. Spirit often is regarded or intuited or perceived as being organized in some way. Various interpretations of this organizing principle lead to the various religions, and so this is as far as the definition of spirituality (attentiveness to spirit) can go without entering the more specified realm of religion. Examples of the organizing principle as it is regarded by different religions are concepts of God (Allah, Great Spirit, etc.) or a group of Gods, a Higher Power more vaguely or impersonally defined, the Tao, the Kami of Shintoism, the Spirit-that-flows-in-all-things of certain Native American traditions, the Void, there are countless others. Also, the degree to which spirit is divisible (e.g., into more or less discrete "spirits") varies according to different religious views.

Forms of Spiritual Experience

Spiritual experiences appear to be universal, regardless of a person's religiosity. Alister Hardy (1979) is a British student of this subject. His book outlines the results of interviews with thousands of people. He and his colleagues were interested in reviewing the results of these interviews to find patterns in which the spiritual aspect of the human being might be seen. "It seems to me that the main characteristics of man's religious and spiritual experiences are shown in his feelings for a transcendental reality which frequently manifest themselves in early childhood; a feeling that 'Something Other' than the self can actually be sensed..." (p. 131).

Hardy found spiritual experiences to be very common, and catalogued and counted their variations. The most common sort of experience was a "sense of security, protection, peace" (on average, 253 mentions per 1000 accounts), followed by "sense of joy, happiness, well-being" (212), "sense of presence (not human)" (202.3), "sense of certainty, clarity, enlightenment" (194.7), visions (181.3), and on through a total of 47 categories. Hardy also looked at circumstances which triggered these experiences. Significant to interpreters is his result that "natural beauty" was one of a group of 4 such triggers that by far dominated the 21 types he listed (the other 3 main ones were "depression, despair;" "prayer, meditation;" and "participation in religious worship"). I'll come back to the significance of beauty, later.

Another student of this topic was Abraham Maslow (1964), the psychologist who developed the pyramid model of human emotional needs discussed in Chapter 6. Maslow was determined to remain within the confines of what he regarded as proper science: "I want to demonstrate that spiritual values have naturalistic meaning, that they...do not need supernatural concepts to validate them, that they...are the general responsibility of all mankind" (p. 4). Like Hardy, Maslow focused on the spiritual experiences of individuals. He concluded that all people have such experiences, whether the person is religious or not. The logical dancing Maslow did to avoid the taint of "supernatural" concepts is rather comical, in my view, but on the whole I think he succeeded in making the point that spiritual questions are important, that they are universal, and that they are the business of public education. Of course, Maslow was careful when defining "spiritual questions." He was willing to acknowledge spiritual feelings and experiences, but chose to explain them in objective, physical terms. Nevertheless we find him pointing out, for example, that a typical characteristic of peak experiences is "that the whole universe is perceived as an integrated and unified whole...and that one has his place in it" (p. 59). There's an interpretive theme for you!

Spirit and Interpretation

Time to come down to Earth. What do we as interpreters do about this? The key for me comes from my own peak experiences, many of them resulting from my practice of advanced awareness techniques (described in Chapter 9). What I have experienced, time after time, are strongly felt spiritual sensations of beauty and of love, perceiving beauty in what conventionally would be called ugly objects or scenes, and feeling love for whatever (or whoever) is in my awareness. I am not alone in focusing on these things. Malone and Malone (1987, p. 247) emphasize that "[t]ruth, beauty, and love are dimensions of reality, not aspects of culture." And here are two similar, significant quotes, one from a religious text and one from an interpretive one:

"The first [commandment] is, ...'you shall love the Lord your God with all your heart, and with all your soul, and with all your mind, and with all your strength.' The second is this, 'You shall love your neighbor as yourself.' There is no other commandment greater than these" (Jesus of Nazareth; The Gospel According to Mark 12:29-31).

"Thus, the six principles with which I began this book may be after all (like the 'single science' mentioned by Socrates) a single princi-

ple. If this should be so, I feel certain that the single principle must be Love" (Tilden 1977, end of chapter 12).

Love ultimately becomes the foundation on which Deep Interpretation is built, and is its endpoint. The community initially is bound together by interdependence, but finally is united by love. The individual starts out as a creature made of stories but ends up as a creature of love. The interpreter begins with a focus on interpretive technique but focuses increasingly on love for what s/he is interpreting and on the love of those for whom s/he is interpreting.

Tilden pointed out that there are no techniques for love and beauty. But the interpreter who lives in beauty and in love will model these things and their appreciation, and thus will teach them, often by what seems to be happy accident rather than design, but make no mistake: this is in fact the most profound spiritual communication. We are in the love and beauty business, as Tilden emphasized. So, love and help others to love. See beauty and help others to find it, in themselves and in the world around them.

Spirit and Storytelling
Now I want to dwell at length on stories, first to emphasize the spiritual aspect of storytelling, then to look at other aspects of stories and their significance in our lives and in determining what we are. No one has summarized the spiritual significance of stories better than the late scholar, Joseph Campbell (1986, 1988). Campbell's life work was the comparative study of myths the world over (by "myth" I mean, here, fundamental stories that shape peoples' world views). Campbell found that myths have common elements and themes, illustrating the unity of our species beneath the more superficial cultural diversity we display.

In his 1986 book, Joseph Campbell outlined how stories can be completely understood only when viewed metaphorically. All stories are about the self, about our individual life journeys. The characters, places and events can be seen as references to different aspects of our selves, the transformations we undergo, the different facets of our personalities, in light and in shadow. Thus, stories and dreams have much in common. The truly powerful and enduring stories, traditional folk tales and stories from ancient religious texts, have these qualities because they speak directly to our subconscious, spelling out the life journeys we are experiencing and placing them in context.

What does this have to do with spirituality? Campbell (1988, p. 229) refers to a Schopenhauer essay which I have been unable to find, so I will rely on Campbell's description. Schopenhauer talks about a common observation that from the perspective of age and experience, one's life seems to have "a consistent order and plan, as though composed by some novelist." Schopenhauer believes that the "novelist" is one's own will, operating often subconsciously. "And just as people whom you will have met apparently by mere chance became leading agents in the structuring of your life, so, too, will you have served unknowingly as an agent, giving meaning to the lives of others. The whole thing gears together like one big symphony, with everything unconsciously structuring everything else." This is the description of a spiritual ecosystem.

Metaphor and myth have power, but care is needed in their use. Peoples' egos, their logical conscious minds, can choose to ignore the more subtle, innate, subconscious grasp of metaphor. As a result, literalism is common. One example is the evolution-creation debate, with scientists on the one hand arguing for a biological explanation of how life has unfolded, and creationists on the other hand arguing for a design effected by a Creator. Much language about hypotheses and theories gets thrown back and forth in this debate, but it seems to me that the debate itself is a facade. These conflicting historical models are substitutes, stalking horses for what in fact is a more fundamental disagreement in myths about what we and the Universe are. Science depends on the myth that there is a division between the natural and the supernatural (some scientists assert that there is no such thing as "the supernatural"), so the story of the Universe can be understood from its own structure and function as determined through physical measurements. The myth of creationism places the physical Universe in a larger context, with extra-physical influences playing a significant role. These influences cannot be measured, only intuited or "revealed." One of these myths has us as biological entities with a long pedigree of genetically developed connections and relationships to the rest of life. The other myth emphasizes a sudden, spiritually based, separately designed appearance of our species. In my opinion, seeing both views as being based on myths helps remove some of the edge from them (remember, I am not using the word 'myth' to mean 'falsehood' here). We are what we are. In the final analysis, isn't that much more important today than how our remote ancestors came to be here?

Spirit and Story in Interpretation

Having said all this, I don't choose to spell out much detail on the application of these ideas about spirit and story in interpretation, other than to point to some topics for your individual thought:

1. We touch the lives of many people, giving them experiences that are stories within the larger stories of their lives. They, in turn, influence the stories we are creating in our own lives.

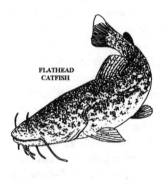

FLATHEAD CATFISH

2. Telling traditional stories is one way of touching on spiritual themes in a powerful, yet subtle and indirect way. It is important to be very selective of the stories, to understand them thoroughly before using them, and to avoid interpreting their symbolism for people. The stories themselves will do the work, subconsciously rather than explicitly.

3. Because of the power of metaphor, any storytelling could be regarded as a spiritual act.

In addition to the many books by Joseph Campbell, three others which examine the metaphoric dimensions of stories, with many examples, are Chopra (1995), Estes (1992) and Meade (1993). The first of these is the one most directly focused on spiritual matters. The stories Chopra interprets are his own, but are based on the King Arthur legend. The other two books are very similar to one another in structure and in the way they interpret traditional stories. They touch on spiritual matters, but are primarily psychological. Estes selected stories with women's growth themes, Meade with men's.

Creating Story Experiences

Now, having addressed some of the esoteric aspects of spirituality, I would like to look at stories at a somewhat more mundane or concrete level. I have become convinced that a large part of education is the creation of stories. I am referring not only to the telling of stories as a teaching technique, but also to the idea of creating stories in the experiences of our students. This notion began to form when I ran across a couple of papers (Loehle 1987, Waldrop 1987) describing how students of human thinking processes were finding that the brain organizes its memories into a library of stories. More recently, applied psychologists (e.g., Bradshaw 1990) have suggested that our story-like memories are fused with the emotions and sensory impressions we experience at each stage in our development. Students of myth (Campbell 1968) and psychologists (Bettleheim 1976) have recognized that traditional stories and myths are metaphors for the individual lives of the listeners. Thus the story should occupy a central role in education. To make all of this clear I should begin with common sense.

Waldrup (1987) reported that computer programmers who wish to create artificial intelligence are trying to understand how common sense works. They find that one element of common sense is the concept of causality. We identify events in relation to each other as causes or effects. The barn burned after the cow kicked over the lantern after the farmer left it behind when he made a sprint to the back house after he ate a meal of something that disagreed with him. Can you read a list of events like that without drawing some conclusions as to causes and effects? Causality is central to story structure.

Causal analysis helps us to make decisions and evaluations. We refer to the stories in our previous experience and compare them to the present situation or problem, asking ourselves: When similar circumstances came up before, what were the consequences? Do I want something similar to happen or something different? That farmer's neighbors likely would say that he didn't use common sense---he failed to see a likely consequence of his leaving the lantern there. Most of the time this is the way we think, and it's very much different from the straight-line logic of a computer.

Common sense also is different from scientific reasoning. This is because common sense depends upon past experience, while science seeks new knowledge. Scientists think up possible cause-and-effect relationships, put them in the form of hypotheses or theories, and test them. The experience comes last instead of first. But there is another way in which science is related to common sense, and it will lead us, as promised, to stories and storytelling.

Loehle (1987) pointed out that ecological systems are so complex that it's difficult simply to test and compare theories. Ecologists seldom get clean, easily interpreted results. So ecologists are especially prone to getting hung up on psychological barriers such as confirmation bias, which is "a tendency to try to confirm one's theory, or not to seek out or use disconfirming evidence." In other words, once a hypothesis is created it gains a momentum of its own. It's easier to remember the results that confirm the hypothesis than those that contradict it.

Theory tenacity is even worse: an emotional attachment to a hypothesis. This one contradicts the basic idea of scientific detachment. But anyone who is a scientist or has worked with them much has witnessed and probably experienced the effects of confirmation bias or theory tenacity. Even when arguments among scientists seem controlled on the surface, underlying tensions can be such that you expect someone to pop out with a "Yo' mamma!" Thus the story-like nature of theories sometimes leads scientists, our society's models of rationality, to reject logic and the weight of evidence for the love of a beautiful story.

OK, so we're not computers, so what else is new? Another way of putting what I've been saying is that we are creatures made up of stories. Whenever we make a decision---whether to turn right on red at a traffic light, whether to believe what a political candidate is telling us, or whether to give credence to a hypothesis (story) explaining small rodent population cycles---we review and compare the relevant stories we have lived. This can be a conscious process or a subconscious one, for example through dreams.

When making judgments we also refer to myths, stories and theories that have been told to us, taking advantage of other people's experiences in similar situations. Storytelling is not simply a lost folk art that is being rediscovered in recent years. Stories saturate our lives. They take the form of movies, TV programs, news reports, and novels. Jokes are stories. If you keep track, you will be impressed by the percentage of casual conversation time that is occupied by storytelling. Sporting events and video games have appeal in part because each contest is a story that unfolds as we watch or participate. Practically all popular entertainments have story form. None of this is surprising if we accept the central role of stories in our mental process.

Here is where storytelling enters an interpreter's bag of tricks. You don't have to moralize with stories. In fact you shouldn't moralize at all. Just select and tell the appropriate tale, and let your listeners be affected by discovering the point(s) for themselves.

When we interpreters guide our students through experiences in the Earth, those experiences become stories in their memories, stories which we hope will come to mind when they are making decisions about how to think, how to live.

Traditional Storytelling

Stories commonly are used by teachers in tradition-based societies. Practically no evolutionary time has passed since the ancestors of every person on Earth lived in traditional societies with tens of thousands of years of background in storytelling. We all have the tools hard-wired into us. We interpreters just have to find and seize them. Stories are interesting enough that we can use them as units without concern about the fact that they lengthen a program. In other words, the time that goes into storytelling is practically negligible when considering audience attention span.

Myths, says Campbell (e.g., 1968, 1989), are the common dream-stories of society. They define our relationships to one another and the Universe. Though the myths of different societies are rich and diverse in detail, Campbell and others have shown that basic themes appear again and again. Campbell uses the term "monomyth" to refer to the universal common denominator. Even the details often are shared. Maui, the mythological hero of New Zealand's indigenous Maori, stole fire from the goddess Mahuika (Dittmer 1907, Best 1925). Coyote, a common trickster figure in stories from indigenous nations of western North America, stole fire from the fireflies in Lipan Apache tradition (Opler 1940). The spirits gave fire to a worthy Mohawk boy in a northeastern story (Tehanetorens 1976). Anyone with much exposure to Greek myths has heard of Prometheus. Fire, being spirit-like, is assigned an unworldly source and so has to have been stolen from spirits or given by gods.

Traditional stories often are thought of as quaint, because they seem designed to "explain" certain familiar features of the natural world. In "The Ball Game of the Birds and Animals" (Chapter 3), two little furry creatures were rejected by the land animals but accepted by the birds, who helped them to gain the air. The bat and flying squirrel used their new wings and gliding skin to help the birds defeat the land animals in a ball game. The purpose of this story is not to "explain" bats and flying squirrels---that is a cultural imposition on our part. We in our science-based society are the ones obsessed with explaining everything. Such stories have the effect of filling the world with mnemonic devices. A child impressed by the story will see a bat in the evening sky, twisting and doubling back like the first bat in that ball game, and will be reminded of the importance of courage, and of the value of even the smallest creature, of even the weakest person. In particular, the small, weak child sees his own value in a world dominated by larger, stronger adults (Bettleheim 1976). The monomyth is the metaphor of our lives.

WHITE-FOOTED MOUSE

Less familiar, but possibly more important in the original cultural context, are traditional stories about places. Their use in teaching is illustrated vividly by Basso (1986). The entire landscape becomes a book, each feature reminding people of what happened to someone whose behavior threatened to undermine the Apache society Basso studied. Basso gives an example he witnessed. A girl violated tradition by wearing her hair in curlers to a ceremony. Two weeks later she was at a party thrown by her grandmother. "And then---quietly, deftly, and totally without warning---her grandmother narrated a version of the historical tale about the forgetful Apache policeman who behaved too much like a white man." The girl soon left the party and went home. The grandmother explained to Basso, "I shot her with an arrow." Two years later Basso asked the girl about it. She said, "I threw those curlers away." When he pointed out the place where the policeman's story had occurred, the girl said, "I know that place. It stalks me every day." Story, landscape, and people become bound together in a web of relationship.

Stories thus can be powerful teaching tools, and storytellers often point out that it is best not to state the moral of the story. For one thing, no really good story has only one lesson, and for another, the lesson is more effective if the student figures it out, as in the example of the Apache girl. This is what I mean by having faith in the fact that we are people made of stories, that we are hardwired story processors. Our subconscious minds take hold of the stories we hear and automatically give us what we need from them.

Inner Child, Inner Adult

But the process by which our brains organize our memories into stories apparently has yet another layer of complexity beyond the simple tying together of events. As we live the stories of our lives, the events are stored along with the sensory impressions and especially the emotional impact they have on us. This is my own reading of the success of the psychological therapy known as inner-child work (Bradshaw 1990, and a number of other popular books, deal with this concept). In the therapeutic applications of this idea, each person is regarded as having a greater or lesser number of emotional needs which were met incompletely in childhood. To the extent that such emotional malnourishment takes place in an individual's life, that person will be stalled, emotionally, at the age where the needs were unmet. Because the needs at each early age are different, different parts of a person's emotional self can be stuck in unhappy holding patterns, exhibiting immature behavior and feeling the child's hurts, seeking subconsciously to get those needs met and achieve full emotional integration and maturity. The therapeutic process seeks to make these subconscious longings conscious. The story of the affected life stage is recalled, relived, viewed from an adult's perspective, and various strategies are employed to fulfill the unmet needs. James Hillman (1979) said that "some of the healing that goes on, maybe even the essence of it, is this collaborative fiction, this putting all the chaotic and traumatic events of a life into a new story."

There are a couple of reasons why I have gone into so much detail about inner-child work. First, it reveals in greater detail how our memories function, supporting the notion that we organize our memories into stories. Second, it points out how complex we are, and how complex are the individuals we are trying to teach. The significance of each teaching transaction becomes magnified when we recognize that the teacher is faced with all the ages of that person at the same time. In the back of my mind, when I am working with children, I realize that the time we are sharing together is being stored in their memories in story form. It is a story that will remain with them through the rest of their lives. Thus, I am not only interacting with the child, but also *with the adult that child will become*. When I am interacting with an adult, I am not only faced with the adult, but *with all the children that adult has ever been*. I am speaking with them all at once! And to the extent that I can enrich the experience with vivid, positive sensory and emotional impressions, I can increase the impact of the story we are living on the subsequent life of the other person.

There are beneficial side effects of this approach, too. First, when I am speaking to the adult that a child will become (keeping in mind the child's developmental learning limitations), I automatically treat the child with the respect he or she deserves. Second, when I remember that the adult before me is carrying her or his inner children along, and I am addressing them all, too, this makes it easier for me to be sensitive to the various needs the person may have, and I let my intuition guide me accordingly. This does not mean that I treat the adult like a child (an idiom which usually means, with less than a full measure of respect). It means being open to play, and concerned for the other's emotional needs at the same time (Robert Fulghum's [1988] famous essay, "All I Really Need to Know I Learned in Kindergarten," sums up this notion succinctly; for a fascinating in-depth view see Paley 1990).

When we guide people through experiences in nature, those experiences become stories in their memories, stories which we hope will influence people when they make decisions about how to think, how to live. The Earthkeepers program (Van Matre and Johnson 1987) creates a larger story and plunges children right into the middle of it. The story features a mysterious, never-seen character named "EM" who is the role-model *par excellence*. When designing a new program, I try to think in terms of the story experience it will create. However you shape the story for your students, their activity and participation is critical. People learn only by doing. But participation can be interpreted broadly in some cases. For instance, listeners to a well-told story are active participants in their imaginations.

Other good elements to include in the story experience are some sort of mystery, problem or challenge to be overcome; vivid sensory impressions; features which enhance participants' self esteem; and a cohesive structure with a beginning, middle and ending.

The best endings are described by the Apache word, Shoona. They have a closure without finality, rooted in the ongoing process of life in the Earth, and spiritually connected to the timelessness of Dreamtime, the eternal mythic world of the story.

Anthropomorphism

One final, specific topic related to storytelling needs to be addressed: anthropomorphism. Anthropomorphism, "an interpretation of what is not human or personal in terms of human or personal characteristics" (Webster's Seventh New Collegiate Dictionary), has become an epithet in interpretive circles. Perhaps the most often cited spook in this particular graveyard is *Bambi*, the Disney movie in which cute little talking animals get blown away by evil hunters. Other headstones bear titles such as "Naming Captive Wild Animals," "Claiming that Animals Experience Emotions," and "Dressing in Animal or Plant Costumes and Pretending to Represent What Those Organisms Are Like." I will now play an interpreter's Igor, exhuming the buried coffins of anthropomorphism and examining their contents for usable pieces.

Anthropomorphism has a time-honored pedigree. Folk tales the world over feature animals that walk, talk and in practically every way behave like human beings while exhibiting particular characteristics. Coyote or Rabbit or Wolverine is a trickster, Spider is sometimes a trickster and sometimes a wise Grandmother, snakes are sneaky and treacherous, turtles are slow but solid and reliable, and other examples are legion. Storytellers, including myself and many other interpreters, tell such stories. One seldom hears objections to this particular form of anthropomorphism.

Why is this phenomenon so widespread among cultures, and what makes these stories so attractive? The answer, I believe, is that we all know that these are stories about people, not stories about animals. More specifically, the animals and other nonhuman characters represent different aspects of human beings, abstracted or converted to metaphors for an entertaining yet enlightening examination. But the characters in these stories are one step removed from actual human beings, which would confuse the issue with their complete humanness. Tellers and listeners can pretend they are talking about animals when in fact they are discussing human weaknesses, foibles, evils and strengths. Stories take place in what indigenous Australians call "dreamtime," the world of the subconscious and of spirit. Stories speak to us subtly without the need for explicit analysis. We don't feel the need to interpret stories, and in fact storytellers are cautioned not to explain their meaning, because a good folk tale has many levels of meaning and thus the potential to convey a different meaning to each hearer. Even children know better than to be confused about real animals, plants or rocks by what they hear in these stories. They do not expect real squirrels, snakes or foxes to speak or behave as they do in folk tales. Yet an encounter with the animal reminds its viewer of the story, acting as a mnemonic device that freshens the story's lesson.

White-tailed Deer
(doe)

What about *Bambi*? What makes that story so different? There are several important differences between the *Bambi* movie and folk tales. First, *Bambi*'s animal characters are too much like individual people. Instead of representing certain human traits or aspects, these characters represent complete personalities. The human characters in the film, in contrast, are one-dimensional. They do not speak. In a traditional tale they might represent people's irrational destructive tendencies. But in the physical world of everyday experience there are people who hunt, so the behavior of the hunters lacks the tension that renders the talking animal characters of folk tales into metaphors. This confuses, and allows viewers to focus on the superficial level of the story, concluding that hunting is bad. People came into *Bambi* grounded in the rules of folk and fairy tales, and because the story did not observe those rules, or perhaps abused them, problematic conclusions were drawn by many viewers.

Thus anthropomorphism per se is not the problem with *Bambi*. The rules of anthropomorphism in stories, if followed consistently, produce powerful lessons. These rules might be summarized as follows: (1) The animal or other non-human characters must display behaviors that clearly are inappropriate for their species, to make it clear that these are not intended to represent the actual animals, plants, rocks, etc. (2) The characters cannot represent complete personalities, but must be abstracted so as to be representative of particular aspects of human beings. Sometimes those aspects may themselves be metaphorical, as in the "magical" powers displayed by some characters. Thus, realistic paintings of dogs playing cards and smoking may not be high art, but they are acceptable anthropomorphism. No one would believe that real dogs would play cards. The dogs in the paintings represent a certain side of male human behavior in a caricatured fashion.

In the Okanagan story of Tick and Deer (Teit et al. 1917, retold below), Coyote represents, among other things, a consciousness of lack while the multi-armed sorcerer represents, among other things, a consciousness of abundance or prosperity. At first, Coyote is in poverty and receives help from the sorcerer. When Coyote

misunderstands the sorcerer's abundance, he tries to kill the sorcerer to steal his wealth. This fails, Coyote learns the lesson and discovers that he, too, has magical powers (i.e., he has metaphorically absorbed the notion of prosperity consciousness). Coyote then uses his powers to give a gift to the sorcerer, transforming him into the first tick, who from then on lives in a world of food and is the embodiment of prosperity (incidentally introducing the story's hearer to a mnemonic in the form of every tick that person subsequently will encounter).

A performance setting has much the same quality as the telling of a folk story. A person putting on an animal costume, especially when that costume is abstracted in some way and the person does not try to mimic the actual animal's behavior too closely, is stepping into the same dreamtime space occupied by folk tales and dreams. It is important, though, that the performer recognize

this, at least semiconsciously. When I wear my abstracted chickadee costume and lead a group of children in my chickadee song
(end of Chapter 12), I am confident that they can easily see that I
am not a bird. While they may be able to recognize a real chickadee from my costume and performance, they will not expect the
bird to speak to them. It is clear that I am a human talking about
chickadees and using the device of the costume and a few abstracted behavior patterns to teach something about chickadees
and, perhaps more importantly, show ways in which chickadees
can teach us positive lessons about how to live our everyday lives.

Do animals have emotions? Behaviorist psychologists have
influenced people into denying this as a possibility, but cannot really demonstrate the nonexistence of emotions in animal experience or consciousness. I am not persuaded by their arguments.
After all, we look at structural homologies between animals and
draw profound conclusions. For instance, the bones of a whale's
flippers are clearly homologous to those of terrestrial mammals'
front limbs. We can follow the evolution of whales from terrestrial
ancestors in the fossil record (Thewissen et al. 1994), confirming
the connection. In a similar way, we see the structure of that part
of the human brain where emotions are centered. We share this
part of the brain stem not only with other mammals but with reptiles. When comparable loci in animals' brains are stimulated elec-
trically they exhibit behaviors which, in humans, would be expres-
sive of emotions (W.R. Hess, E.v. Holst and U.v.Saint-Paul, as described by Eibl-Eibesfeldt 1970). It seems much more reasonable
to me to accept the possibility, or even likelihood, of emotionality
in animals in the face of such observations, than to deny it out-
right. We simply have to be cautious about asserting that a particular human emotion is being expressed by a particular animal in a
particular situation. But cautious speculation seems safe to me as
long as it is understood and labeled as such. For more detail on
these points, see Rumbaugh (1994).

Finally, what about the practice of naming captive wild animals? This sometimes is frowned upon because it is assumed that
this makes the animals seem like pets, or even people
(anthropomorphism). There are good lessons to be taught with
such naming, however. Names point to the uniqueness of the individual, are an aspect of particularization. This uniqueness is as true
in animals as it is in us. I am much less comfortable with the typo-
logical thinking (a red-tail is a red-tail is a red-tail) that results from

the religious avoidance of naming than I am with naming that respects the individuality of a particular bird. Care must be used, however, to allow the red-tailed hawk to be a red-tailed hawk and to represent it as such, and not as one's little feathered but otherwise human buddy.

In summary I find most anthropomorphism to be harmless. Used properly, especially according to the deeply rooted conventions of folk tales, anthropomorphism can be a powerful teaching tool. We need to be clear in our own minds about the differences between the entities of the wild as metaphors and as beings in their own right with their own, non-human qualities. An interpreter who is clear about these differences should be able to walk through the graveyard of anthropomorphism without needing to whistle.

Enough talking about stories. Let's get to one, my re-telling of a folk tale from Teit et al. (1917).

Tick and Deer (Okanagan)

It was the middle of winter, and the mountains and valleys of the Pacific Northwest were covered by a deep layer of the whitest snow. Only a few things were tall enough to stick out of that snow. There were the spruces and firs, for instance, which seemed to huddle together in little clusters in the cold. And there also, at the foot of the mountain, was Coyote's tent.

Inside, Coyote was starving. He had run out of food, and there was no chance of getting more in that deep snow. Coyote was warm enough, though. He lay curled up by his fire. He was thinking about all the good food he had ever eaten.

"Oh, I wish. How I wish I had...just some nice soup bones, with maybe a little meat on them..."

Whump! There was a loud sound outside his tent door, as if someone (or something) had fallen into the snow. Slowly Coyote opened his tent door and peeked out. Why, there was a bag lying in the snow. Coyote looked all around, but could see no one. He went out and picked up the bag. It was made of soft, brain-tanned deerskin and in it were soup bones, just like he had wished for.

Coyote took those bones back inside and cooked them up. His soup lasted several days. But then it ran out, and before long, Coyote was starving again.

"Oh, I wish. How I wish I had some more of those soup bones, maybe with some chunks of meat besides..."

Whump! The same sound as before. Coyote immediately got up and opened the tent door. There was no one to be seen, but there was another deerskin bag, and in it were more soup bones, and some chunks of meat besides.

Again Coyote was saved. But now, as he savored this food over the next several days, Coyote began to wonder where these gifts were coming from. If he could find out, he would have an unending supply of food.

He waited until this food was gone, and he fasted until he was good and hungry again. Then he lay with his nose just beside the tent door and he wished: "Oh, I wish. How I wish I had more of those soup bones, with some chunks of meat and some fat, besides."

Whump! Coyote immediately looked out the door. He was just in time to see someone disappearing from sight. He had just a glimpse, but that was enough to tell him who it was. It was a little man, a wizard, who had been misformed by many extra arms which grew out of his body.

After Coyote had finished the food and was hungry again, he followed the wizard's tracks all the way to the top of the mountain. There he saw the little man's camp: a tent, surrounded by racks upon racks of drying deer meat. There were piles of bones, and the skins were all on stretchers. Coyote entered the tent, and found the wizard warming his back by the fire.

"Say, I really appreciate all that food you've been giving me. But I hate to have you carry it all the way to my tent. Could I move in here with you? Then I could help you with things, carry water and the like."

The wizard looked at Coyote's skinny, mangy body and said, "Well, Coyote, I'm not sure I really care to have a coyote living in my tent. But you may move your camp up here next to mine, if you wish."

Coyote moved his camp, and began to work for the wizard and to share his food. But the work became tedious after a couple of days. Besides, Coyote could see that there was not enough food in the wizard's camp to feed them both for the rest of the winter. "If I could get rid of him, I would have plenty of meat for myself."

So the next day, when the little man went out for a walk, Coyote followed him. When he came to a pile of rocks, Coyote took one, hit him over the head with it, and then proceeded to pound him flat, so that all those arms stuck out to the sides. Coyote tossed him into the brush and turned back toward camp.

But as soon as Coyote came within view of the tents, he saw the most amazing thing. The piles of bones were jumping up and assembling themselves into deer skeletons. Then the meat leaped off the drying racks and slapped itself onto the skeletons. Finally, the skins untied themselves from the stretchers and covered the deer, who were now whole again. They ran past Coyote toward the place where he had left the wizard. Coyote realized the wizard was still alive, and had resuscitated the deer.

Coyote ran after them, saying, "Wait! You're my dinner!" He got to the rock pile just in time to see the wizard grab the tail of the last deer and be carried away. Coyote knew he had been defeated, and he found that he had the power to turn the little man into a tiny creature, flattened and tough with many arms sticking out to the sides, who always would have the deer to live on. So Coyote created the tick, and we have them still today.

As for Coyote, he had to find another way to get through that winter. And so he headed back to his camp, up over the hill and into another story.

A more comprehensive interpretation: Coyote at the beginning of the story represents lack, but also desire. He expresses that desire, and his need is filled, but only temporarily. He is in a womb-like hut, then. The food arrives from outside, drawing his attention that way. He glimpses something, a new idea, represented by the sorcerer. The sorcerer represents prosperity consciousness. He lives high on the hill, and can see the abundant world all around him. He does not stay in his hut, but goes out each day to partake of that abundance and to share it (e.g., with Coyote). He leaves tracks: anyone can follow his example. Coyote takes the first step of birth, emerging from his hut and going to the sorcerer's camp. Coyote talks to the sorcerer but does not understand him. The sorcerer sees Coyote's poverty and knows Coyote is not ready to share his tent. He allows Coyote to move closer, however; he has learned, and earned, that much. Coyote has indeed progressed. He no longer simply takes, he is of a mind to trade his work for food. This is not yet prosperity thinking, which would be giving to participate in the Universe's abundant flow. At the same time, Coyote's level of understanding leads him to count up the sorcerer's stock in hand and, not understanding its source, assumes that there is inadequate food to sustain the two of them for the winter. Again he follows the sorcerer, but instead of taking advantage of the opportunity to learn from him, Coyote hits him with a rock, pounds him flat (sees him only in 2 dimensions), and throws him in the brush. If the sorcerer were of Coyote's consciousness he would be dead, but even there in the brush tangle with his body broken, the sorcerer maintains his sense of prosperity. The fruits of the sorcerer's abundance being a product of his consciousness, the deer re-assemble themselves and go to him. Coyote, dismayed, runs after them. He sees them rescue the sorcerer. Finally Coyote understands, and demonstrates his understanding with his own first act of prosperity: he gives the sorcerer a new form that forever will be the epitome of abundance, and furthermore will serve as an example to us, if we are open to the idea of learning from a tick.

An alternative interpretation: Remember that any good story is open to more than one interpretation. Here, Coyote is getting his needs met, but he's not satisfied. He has to delve into the mechanism. In the end, it gets him in trouble. This could be taken as a cautionary point about over-analyzing things (such as stories).

Part 3: The Circle of the Interpreter

Part 3: The Circle of the Interpreter

Freeman Tilden gave us a definition of interpretation, but he emphasized that each interpreter must define interpretation for him/herself. In my model, the interpreter's circle (*Fig. 4*) is the smallest, the least important, of the three. Our egos want us to take center stage, and certainly we are a conspicuous presence, but I hope that what we really want is for the members of our audiences to develop their own, personal and strongly felt attachment to the resource we are interpreting. This attachment is based both on understanding (i.e., is cognitive) and feeling (i.e., is affective). If it is dependent on us, it is too weak to last. The real bond of significance in this entire model, the true measure of our success, is the bond between our human constituents and the resource. "Thou shalt not inflict interpretation," a commandment I first heard from National Park Service interpreter Robert Fudge, is relevant here.

The outside of the interpreter's circle is a quartet of inputs and outputs, which at first may seem mechanical and abstract, like a flow chart. Each of these four elements is complex and dynamic, requiring much study and practice to be well developed. The study of awareness techniques enables us to keep in touch with our surroundings from moment to moment. When we are aware of the current state of what is going on around us, both in the resource and in the audience, we can pick and choose from the variety of teachable moments that constantly is in reach. We can seek to touch each person with whatever she or he needs from us and from the landscape, to enhance their own capacity for awareness and to bond with the resource, as my adult friends did when pointing out herons and owls to me when I was a child.

The most fundamental and important form of interpretive output is modeling. The interest and feeling we display for the resource demonstrates its value, its worthiness for study and heartfelt attachment. Other interpretive outputs such as program and exhibit design, and verbal communication in its various forms, are crafts which take careful study to master. All of them have psychological, intellectual and spiritual subtleties which fascinate me, and which are elaborated in this book.

It is easy, especially early in an interpreter's career, to get caught up in these techniques. This is not bad. Mastery isn't achieved all at once, and total mastery seldom, if ever, is achieved by anyone. We all are learning. The details of the craft, and the mass of knowledge base regarding the resource, are daunting when first encountered. We often focus on these things. The audience remains that, an "audience," a single body with many heads. It's too much to ask that we recognize all those individuals.

But, just as the center of the community circle becomes transmuted from interdependence to love, and the individual grows from story to love, so too does the interpreter evolve, I believe, from an overwhelmed focus on knowledge and technique to a love of the community and particularly of the individual people for whom (with whom) we are interpreting. Knowledge and technique never disappear, but with mastery they become transparent, a breathable atmosphere that connects interpreter with audience members. Methods become subordinate, almost trivial in importance, compared to the relationship between the interpreter and audience, which in turn is, again, less important than the relationship between the people and the resource. Ideally that relationship best can be described as a form of love.

One important aspect of "nature" interpretation is its function in opening peoples' hearts to the voices of the Earth. The idea here is that we are not so different from language interpreters. The language we interpret for people is the resource itself. Ultimately the interpreter must stand aside and let the beauty of this language, as the person now understands it, speak for itself in a dialogue which will enrich the person's life and add value to the resource. The interpreter, witnessing this, can be reminded of the process by which the resource captured her or his own heart on the beginning of the path that led to this point.

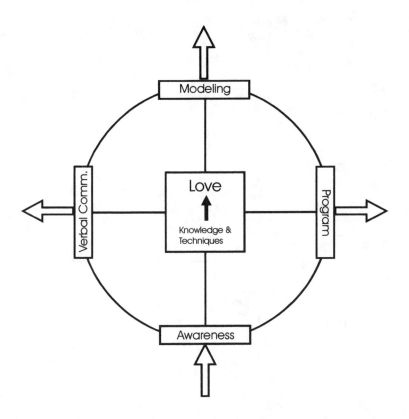

Figure 4: The Circle of the Interpreter

Chapter 9: Awareness

Introduction

Several years ago I led a winter nature walk which took us along a stream where a pair of great horned owls were territorially active. An elderly woman had shown herself to be remarkably aware, seeing many things I had missed. I welcomed her observations, and marveled at her ability. She even picked out the owls before I saw them. At the time I did not know that the way to see an owl is not to look for an owl, but to see the entire forest. Then awareness of the owl comes automatically.

A couple of winters later, after having begun to study advanced awareness techniques, I was tracking a red fox through another forest. I had been following him for more than a hundred yards, my head down, searching for every footprint, when I felt a pressure on the right side of my head. I rotated my neck to face the direction from which the pressure was coming, and found myself looking into the seeming outraged eyes of a great horned owl on the nest. Now, have you had the experience of feeling that you were being watched? At such times you are using what I call an advanced awareness technique. There are steps that can be taken to improve awareness, not only to increase the number of things that we notice, but also to enhance our appreciation of their beauty. The purpose of this chapter is to introduce some of these techniques, and provide exercises that can help us to develop them. I also will suggest some applications in interpretive work.

I don't claim to be aware all the time. But given my starting point, I've made a lot of progress. I'm not interested in competing, only in improving my ability, and even if you are basically more aware than I am I hope you will find some ideas of value here. Ultimately the techniques fuse, becoming one technique of awareness. But they are learned one at a time.

Relaxation Techniques

A prerequisite for awareness is relaxation. Relaxation allows us to slow down and tune out everything but the process of awareness. Awareness requires us to let go of worries, of concerns about time, of thoughts of what we are going to do next. Different people use different techniques to "get into the woods." One of these is physical: tighten the voluntary muscles, hold the tension for a few seconds, then release. When we are learning it helps to focus on one group of muscles at a time (e.g., those of the feet, then the legs, then the lower torso, etc.), then work our way up to doing it all at once. This technique works by catching up any subtle muscular tensions of which we may be unaware, then deliberately releasing them.

Other, more mental techniques, include listening to relaxing music. Sometimes I like to do a mental countdown, slowing down mentally as I approach "zero," having trained myself in this way to relax, to become a part of the world around me. Another relaxation method I have used is to create a poem or phrase that will act as a reminder or trigger for awareness. For instance: "Let your shell of troubles collapse to the forest floor, and step away from it./ Now take the reality of each leaf and wrap it around you." Meditation techniques also facilitate relaxation. They, like the others, have the physical effect of slowing brain waves, resulting in increased awareness and learning capacity. One of my favorites is a breathing meditation: I close my eyes and imagine that I am breathing in the world around me, then breathing out my consciousness or awareness or attentiveness so as to spread it through the surrounding world.

Types of Awareness Techniques

The relaxation process prepares us for the awareness techniques themselves. Some of these are sensory techniques, relatively straightforward uses of the conventional senses. Sensory techniques have the greatest appeal to those whose learning styles are geared to sensory input and attention to the physical surroundings. Other techniques are intuitive techniques, and will have the greatest appeal to those whose learning styles include looking inside themselves for information about what is going on around them. A third category contains composite techniques that are made up of both sensory and intuitive components.

Wide-Angle Vision

The first of the sensory techniques is wide-angle vision. Communications technologies such as print and television have provided many advantages necessary for the development of our civilization. But there have been costs, too, and one of these is the way we use our sense of vision. Television screens are small, and a line of print occupies an even tinier portion of our visual field. These media train us to focus our vision narrowly, to look at only one small thing at a time. But when we do so, we miss most of what is going on around us. We use our vision like a flashlight

GREAT
HORNED OWL

beam illuminating the eyes of an animal at night. Everything else is darkness. The preferred alternative is to spend most of our time in wide-angle vision (Brown 1983). A person using wide-angle vision loses some detail, but there is nothing wrong with focusing narrowly for a short time, or for as long as is necessary. By seeing widely we see more, notice more.

Conventional, narrow vision is allied to the linearity of language. Notice how impossible it is to describe ecosystems in strings of words. Wide-angle vision, considering many parts of an ecosystem at once in parallel, opens the door to a better understanding of how ecosystems really function. Wide-angle vision is especially sensitive to movement, and is necessary for optimal seeing in dim light. This is because when we are focusing narrowly, we are using the fovea, small regions in our retinas composed almost entirely of cones, which do not function in dim light. With wide-angle vision we use the entire retina, which also has rods, the receptors for light intensity. When I teach this technique to kids, sometimes I'll use the rabbit as an example of an animal who uses wide-angle vision. It is a great method for grabbing teachable moments. For example, while presenting a firefly program one evening, I caught movement above, and the result was that I was able to show people some black-crowned night herons, a species then on the Illinois Endangered Species List, as they flew over. Another outcome of learning this technique is that I seldom use binoculars, anymore. They entrain narrow vision too much.

Here's a way to discover wide-angle vision (Brown 1983, p. 40). Spread your arms straight out to the sides, stretching them until your hands are slightly behind the plane of your face. Point your eyes straight forward, and switch into wide-angle vision (i.e., don't focus on any particular thing, but rather diffuse your attentiveness over your entire field of view). Wiggle the fingers of both hands, and slowly move your arms forward until you see the movement (there will be no detail) in the corners of both eyes simultaneously. Your arms still should be nearly straight out to the sides. Move your hands around the edges of your visual field, continuing to point your eyes straight ahead, to define the large area covered by wide-angle vision. Once you've discovered it, try to practice seeing in wide-angle vision most of the time. Pay attention to movement, check it out with temporary narrow vision, then switch back into wide-angle vision. Over time it will become automatic (people who make this a goal commonly achieve it within 6 weeks). In this as in all advanced awareness techniques, relaxation and an unhurried internal pacing are needed. Practicing wide-angle vision while watching TV puts the box in its place, as a small feature out of your total surroundings. Practicing wide-angle vision while driving or walking city streets improves safety.

3-D Vision

The second physical awareness technique also is visual: seeing in three dimensions. We all know that our physical universe has three dimensions of space, but thanks to our current dependence on one-dimensional print and two-dimensional TV and movies, many of us don't actually see in three dimensions. A demonstration of this is that people often look at the surface of a mass of vegetation, say a forest or clump of brush, without seeing into or through it, without noticing the three dimensional arrangement of the plants. But back in there is where most of the action is. One of the first methods I used to break into 3-D vision was to watch individual trees while riding in a car in winter (as a passenger, not as driver). I noticed how the trees seemed to turn, rotating around their trunks. I found my mind automatically building 3-D images of them. Another step was to take a walk through a woods or, even better, a brushy area, letting my mind derive the 3-D picture of the scene. I found that I could see it more easily, at first, if I watched a small area continuously as I walked. If you try this, remember to look into or through the area, not just at its surface. Snorkeling and diving enhance 3-D vision, in part because even clear water is less transparent than air, exaggerating the dimension of depth, and in part because for a time you are a creature moving in all three dimensions, and need to attend to all of them. My interpretive analogy when introducing this technique to kids is the penetrating vision of the hawk.

Importance of Sounds

We'll come back to vision, but now I want to focus on sounds. The first point about hearing is that every sound, even the smallest and faintest, is significant in a natural setting. Deer teach this. On several occasions, watching deer who did not know I was there, I was struck by how sensitive they were to the slightest sounds. The small snap of a twig, barely noticeable to me, would stop a deer from feeding for several minutes while it peered in the direction from which the sound had come, sniffing and moving its ears to obtain more information. Out of this lesson I have profited many times by seeking the sources of little sounds. Focused hearing (Brown 1983, p. 50) helps. Cup your hands behind your ears. The optimal positioning of your bent arms is about 45 degrees to either side of straight forward. There are two applications of focused hearing. To amplify sounds, point both ears straight forward. To locate the direction from which a sound is coming, take a lesson from the owls and tilt one ear up, one down. Once, while on a bird walk at a place called Chaa Creek in Belize, we heard a hooting call which our guide identified as belonging to a motmot. We were about to plunge into the brush to seek it, but with focused hearing I was able to locate the bird and save us the trouble. The tropical forests teach, though, that complex reflecting surfaces create difficulties. The technique requires a direct line-of-hearing between you and the sound source.

Scanning

The third dimension includes us. We need to be aware of what is all around us, not just in front of us, and to include ourselves in the environment. Scanning is a technique for accomplishing this. We need to turn our eyes to all directions, in wide angle vision, and with 3-D vision keep track of all depths as well. As in wide angle vision, you will see more animals (for instance) as you gain control of the techniques. It's not entirely automatic, though. You will need experience, for example, to see that there is a rabbit when only the outer half of one ear is in view. In time you learn to see the distinctive shapes and colors of parts of the different animals. I find that if circumstances have kept me out of the woods for a time, scanning is a good starting point for restoring awareness. A way to get into this technique is to maintain focus by imagining that at every instant there is a mouse within 3 feet, a rabbit within 30 feet and a Great Horned Owl within 100 yards, and you wish to see them all(juggle animals and distances as habitats and your preferences demand). If you do Scanning right, you will find that it requires you to slow down. If you insist on seeing everything, you are forced to stop and spend a long time in one place before taking a step. You not only turn all around, but you also stretch up, crouch down, move in ways that allow you to see around obstructions, etc.

Proximity Sense

One of the most amazing demonstrations of awareness I have seen was performed by a master of Japanese swordsmanship. He was both blindfolded and wearing a thick, densely woven hood of black fabric. He found his way into a quartet of people, some of them his students, one a volunteer from the audience (I was one of the students). Each of us held a cucumber before us, angling them as we chose. He drew his sword and cut thick-potato-chip slices from each of our cucumbers in turn, about a second's time separating each cut. Another teacher, Tom Brown, Jr., took my group of students out half a mile from camp one night, had us blindfold ourselves, and told us to make our way back through the woods to camp, following the sound of a drum that was being pounded by an instructor. We found that we could somehow feel the spaces between the trees and go to them after a couple of encounters with trunks. By the time we made it back to camp, we could feel masses of brush and avoid them, as well. We were using an additional sense, called proximity sense by some, which gives us information about nearby physical objects and spaces. At first, most people find spaces easier to identify confidently than objects. This is easier to do with massive objects like trees than with smaller ones.

Gut Feeling

The most practical of the intuitive techniques is gut feeling. It involves paying attention not only to sensations from without, but those within. You are part of the landscape through which you are moving. In most people, some impressions are registered indirectly, not in the brain but projected into the gut. I find that gut feelings confirm or deny my conclusions, my choices. This is one form of intuition, an important foundation for awareness that we in our European-derived, rational society have neglected. Once people get around the brain's ability to mimic the feeling, and use it purely, they find it a great awareness tool. Photographer Dewitt Jones (1988) wrote, "I sometimes get a very strong push to be somewhere at a particular time, and usually when I follow this urge, something magical happens." Jones shared an anecdote of a gloomy, hopeless day when he was pushed by gut feeling to make a long drive and climb up Sentinel Dome in Yosemite. A narrow line of sky at the horizon produced a beautiful sunset and his first spread in National Geographic. "I'm writing about it because, in truth, it's far more central to my photography than any tip I could give you about filters and f-stops."

Gut feeling can be used in several ways, and could be regarded as at least 3 separate techniques. One is a general feeling or impression of the surrounding landscape, which can be refined to the sense of what is happening in it. The first time I visited the tropics was a month-long visit to Panama, part of a graduate course in tropical ecology. I was intimidated. Everything was so diverse, so big (for instance, walking sticks with bodies as thick as, and longer than, large stick pretzels). By my second tropical trip, this time to Belize, I had some grounding in awareness. I was surprised to find that the gut feeling of a tropical forest was very similar to that of forests back home. It was less scary, then.

A more specific use of gut feeling is to answer a particular question, say about the location of something. I have used it to locate people in crowds, to find lost objects, to find animal signs. Narrow the process to a series of yes-no questions. Is it in this direction? That? Is it 100 yards away? Less? Feel for tension or a warning away, which indicates "no," versus a feeling of relief or relaxation of tension, indicating "yes."

Finally, there is the use of gut feeling in making decisions. "Follow your bliss" was a favorite expression of Joseph Campbell, and could be used to describe this application of gut feeling. I depend upon it for my most important decisions. The way I use it is to envision myself taking each alternative choice, and examine gut feeling for warnings or attractions. This method has proven its value more times than I can remember.

Other Forms of Intuition

When profound relaxation and practice in intuition are combined, remarkable experiences can result. I was walking a trail in the Morton Arboretum, a wonderful private-foundation-run area in my county, a few years ago. I crossed a dry streambed and followed a trail that ran 15 yards above it. I was contemplating a beautiful oak when I got a message, as though someone were speaking in my head, to hold very still, as a large animal was coming toward me along the streambed. A minute or so later I saw a glimpse of it, in the distance, a yellow color to its fur. Soon it was passing below me, a red fox with a dead chipmunk in its mouth. It reached the place where I had crossed the streambed a few minutes earlier, turned around, and quickly went back the way it had come.

Sometimes intuition makes use of metaphors. I was building a survival shelter for demonstration purposes in a brushy area of the Willowbrook Wildlife Center. I had been taking my time, doing it right without visibly damaging the landscape, and it had taken all day. I was carrying an armload of leaves for bedding, still out of sight of the shelter, when my eye was drawn to a bit of litter, a broken piece of black plastic shaped like a claw. I had the impression that something described by that plastic was at my shelter. I had visions of some black-leather-clad vandal, and very quietly wound my way through the last 50 yards of footpath. Then I had to laugh. A black cat was investigating the shelter. This cat had been a frequent visitor to the forest preserve for over a year, but was so aware and so stealthy that except for a handful of sightings, I knew it mainly by its tracks. The insulation of the shelter had masked my approach, and when I started to laugh, the cat practically turned itself inside out running away.

Other impressions are more vague, as in the owl story I told at the beginning of this chapter. I don't pretend to be able to explain these experiences completely. I believe they are beyond complete explanation in rational terms.

The Whole Landscape

The Whole Landscape is a term I use for the combination of physical and intuitive techniques, applied to the surroundings as a whole. We need to treat all the senses the way we've been treating vision. It's time to hear, smell, feel in the three dimensions, out to the limits of the landscape, in wide angle, i.e., in all directions at once. Maintaining The Whole Landscape for even 1/2 hour can produce a sense of magic, because it opens you to the touch of a place's spirit. Hearing, scanning, moving slowly and gut feeling are the most important contributing elements.

One of the less complicated variations on the Whole Landscape technique is attending to the concentric rings. I practice this one by sitting in one place for 20 minutes or more at a time. I soak in my surroundings through all my senses. I find myself noticing both specifics of animal activities and poorly defined impressions. Both turn out to be real and important. Both silences and sounds convey the landscape's heartbeat. If you try this one, I recommend that you return to your spot at different times of day, under different conditions. Also, try other spots.

Seeing Purely

Seeing purely is the single awareness technique I value most. The idea is to postpone labeling, naming, making critical evaluations, even recognizing, what you perceive. Turn off your sensory filters and take it all in. See a thing or event for what it is, see all that it is, let it define itself through its own particulars. Prolonging the arrival of the moment of recognition allows more detail to be absorbed. When you look at a bird or a squirrel, do you simply see "bird" or "squirrel," or can you remove the labels and see every hair and feather, the uniqueness of that being?

Most people who have spent much time outdoors have experienced seeing purely in at least one way. Imagine that it is night, and you are gazing at a beautiful starry sky. Suddenly, unexpectedly, a streak of light zips across your field of view and is gone. Because you could not anticipate it, because it caught you totally by surprise and happened so quickly, there was a moment in which you saw it purely, before your brain caught up and attached the label/concept "meteor." What did you feel in that moment of purity?

As a deliberate technique, seeing purely is not easy to learn. The first step is to understand that it can be done and to set it as a goal. You know you are beginning to succeed when you discover the Oriental concept of the 10,000 Things. For me, it first happened as I walked across a winter corn field with all the stalks knocked down. I looked at the ground and suddenly that entire little scene filled my visual field. I saw the beauty and particularness of each bit of each cornstalk. At the same time I absorbed the spatial relationships of all those bits, all those cornstalks, and that was beautiful, too. The sense of beauty did not come in the instant of seeing purely, but in the next instant, as the first critical thought. It came automatically. The next thought was the realization that this is what is meant by the 10,000 Things. So by having heard about the possibility, and wanting to experience it, I had set myself up for its eventually taking place.

My favorite objects of seeing purely are broadleafed trees. Each one has its own shape, its own individuality, which best can be appreciated by applying this method. Instead of seeing the tree as a whole, see the leaves, all of them, each of them, and the twigs and branches, all of them, each of them with its particular twists and turns. Do so in wide angle vision, so that you are seeing them all at once. If you can pop out of the tree concept and see the tree purely, you will know it immediately, through the wonderful feeling and the sense of insight. Seeing the tree purely, especially in winter with its leaves off, allows a form of comprehension of the tree's life dance that gave it this shape. Typically you'll see it purely for a portion of a second, then pop out of it with an insight or focal point that summarizes or represents an aspect of the tree.

The usual result is to achieve pure vision for only a moment at a time. That's OK; it is common to see purely for a moment, to register some insightful profit-taking, then to dive back into seeing purely, and continue alternating between the two states. I have the greatest difficulty with faces. There is too much going on, too much social cogitating, for it to be easy. The feeling outcome is identical, though, underlining our equivalence to all else in nature. Additional technique is needed. You need the courage to be yourself in the presence of the other person, to be unafraid of hurting the person or being hurt by them. Then, you must be able to look at the person in the same way you do, say, a tree you are seeing purely. You must allow that person to be himself or herself, free of any conclusions you may have drawn about him or her. As with the tree, you will come out of the pure seeing with some focal clue or feature to build on.

Seeing purely allows us to absorb the details of a scene but not simultaneously to interpret its meaning. And even when we begin to conceptualize what is before us after seeing purely, we do not comprehend it totally. You may look into a patch of brush and see a hidden rabbit, having learned to recognize the end of its ear, but you may fail to notice the clues as to which runway it used to reach that position. You may not know how to read the biogra-

phies of the different shrubs surrounding the rabbit, biographies recorded in the plants' structure. You might miss the toad sitting a couple of feet to the right of the rabbit, the moth resting on the leaf above it, etc. But I have found that with practice and experience, and by diving back into pure vision repeatedly to glean all I can from a scene, I obtain more and more from each experience.

Another application of seeing purely is to use it when watching a person, or group of people, or an animal in motion. This even works with TV---sporting events or dance performances are especially good. Again, watch without labeling or worrying about what they are doing or why they are doing it. As you begin to succeed you will notice more detail, because when you are not being impeded by the processes of filtering and labeling, you are seeing it all. When watching a bird in flight and seeing purely, my mind can register the detail of each wingbeat, each little turn of head and tail. Once I was watching Olympic pairs skaters performing, and spent as much time as possible seeing them purely. I found I identified one pair as being in love. They proved to be the only ones who kissed when their program ended. Once I spent an enraptured 5 minutes in a barn in front of a naked lightbulb. The dance of the dust particles, viewed in pure vision, had me entranced. Now I understand infants when they are doing the same.

Emergent Consequences of Awareness

I have found that practicing these awareness techniques leads
to certain emergent patterns with profound consequences on my
view of things. Nearly all of these techniques share certain features.
They open me up, open me out, cause me to become interdigi-
tated with my surroundings. I extend into the landscape and absorb it into me. A central paradox of advanced awareness is that
the techniques succeed to the extent that the ego disappears. What
fills the gap, communicating beautifully with the little of me that is
left, is something I call "The Enraptured Witness." New Thought
philosophies have a term "Higher Self" which seems to be the
same thing. Once I stood and watched as hundreds of sandhill
cranes flew into a field, part of a migratory staging area in northern
Indiana, after a foraging trip. The sky was filled with them, and the
sound of their massed calls was so loud and amazing that my ego
diminished to the point where only a wonderfully witnessing small
self remained. Again, I don't accept this at face value simply because it is a far out idea. In the real, physical, nuts and bolts world,
the more I lose ego, the more I perceive, the more animals I see,
the more significant details I notice, and the more rapture I feel.
The ego, through its sensory filters, blocks us from complete
awareness.

Take this for what you find it to be worth: I get better results,
see more animals, etc., when I love the landscape and all its parts,
and acknowledge them to be alive. Awareness then becomes a
form of communication. I'm not sure it's possible to see purely
without love being involved, for instance.

And the ultimate, the farthest point I've been able to reach so
far with physical awareness, has come through a spiritual notion.
People who live close to the Earth, people who cultivate awareness, commonly have notions of a Creator, or at least some form
of sentient creative force or plan. The Earth belongs to and is the
physical manifestation of that Creator, i.e., the Creator is a spiritual
being, mainly, but has a body as well. That body is all the Earth,
all the physical Universe. In that view, every individual animal,
plant, rock, tree and person is not simply one of the 10,000
things---it is one of the 10,000 fingers of God. All things are exten-
sions or expressions of a single entity, a Whole. The Hindu
prayer-greeting, bowing toward another person with the hands
held in a prayerful position, is an acknowledgement of this universal divinity. The notion gives an added perspective on how Native

142

Americans and other peoples who live close to the Earth come by their great respect.

With practice, awareness techniques teach that landscapes are holographic: each part reflects, represents, in a sense contains, the whole. Taken to the extreme, this notion allows me to approach some object, see it purely, and say, "You are God." In my experience the feeling that accompanies this pronouncement is a rapturous sense of profound, non-verbal communication.

Tracking

That summarizes the techniques, but I wish to include the art of tracking in this chapter, as well. It is a language as much as an application of awareness techniques, but within the model of interpretation I am presenting in this book, tracking has the place of providing another input that the interpreter can use.

In 1989, when the National Interpreters' Workshop was in Minnesota, I had a hair-raising experience at the natural history museum in St. Paul. In one of the lower corridors there was an exhibit showing a set of fossilized footprints from a long-extinct species of shorebird. An artist's educated guess of the bird's appearance accompanied the fossil. The tracks were preserved in a siltstone that showed them clearly. As my eyes moved from footprint to footprint, my tracking experience kicked in and I felt goosepimples rising. I was envisioning the detailed movements, the nervous little prehistoric dance on an ancient mud flat, of a bird which last had drawn breath eons ago.

Tracking is the study of changes in landscapes. These changes may be large or small in scale, but always they reflect upon the landscape as a whole. Tracking is an attitude as much as it is an art. The tracker studies the details of the surroundings, putting them together to reconstruct the activities of animals, the growth of plants, and the influence of physical forces. Instead of focusing on the static details of a footprint or the shape of a tree, the tracker uses these clues for reconstructions, imagining and extrapolating to connect those events to other things happening in the landscape.

Everything that happens changes the world in some way, and leaves clues that allow us to reconstruct those changes. When we teach ourselves to look for such clues, and to read from them the stories they tell, they can give us a direct, experiential connection to the past and thus enrich our appreciation of how the present came to be the way it is. Any object can provide these clues---I shall give examples of three common ones: footprints, trees and landforms.

The best trackers can read every detail of an animal's condition and movements from the minute disturbances of the soil within and around the tracks. Tom Brown, Jr., writes (1983, p. 112): "Tracking produces a kind of communion. Each clue draws you closer to the being that left it. With each discovery, your own tracks become more deeply entwined in the mystery you are following. Eventually, you absorb so many clues that the mystery and its answer are bound up inside you. The animal comes alive in your imagination. You can feel it moving, thinking and feeling long before you come to the end of the string." While few reach such an elevated level in the tracking art, there are so many enjoyable lessons along the way that any degree of tracking skill is worth obtaining.

Tracking is a language, and the best trackers are highly sophisticated linguistic interpreters. But any language begins with its alphabet, and the species identification of clear footprints is the alphabet of tracking. The next step after footprint identification is to learn how different kinds of animals walk, and how these differences translate into patterns of footprints (Brown 1983).

For instance, wide-bodied animals like bears and raccoons walk in the pace gait, swinging their bodies from side to side as they move both of their left feet at the same time, then both right feet. A pacing animal leaves side-by-side pairs of footprints, the front foot from one side of the body registering beside the hind foot from the other side. Other animals walk in other gaits, each resulting in a different arrangement of footprints. Once the gaits are understood, the student of tracking pursues finer details within the prints which reveal the age of the track, and a more complete picture of what the animal was doing when it made the track.

A somewhat longer timespan can be investigated through tree tracking. The first rule of tree tracking is that a tree's trunk and branches grow toward light and away from shade, becoming fixed in place as they grow. The second rule is that well-shaded branches are allowed to die and fall off. The third rule is that the diameter of a stem or branch increases with age. These three rules enable us to interpret many stories. A tree with a lean in its trunk often is witness to the presence of an older tree which shaded it on one side in its youth. Such a tree can indicate the ghostly presence of the older tree, now dead, even if all traces of the older one have rotted away.

A thick-trunked tree with many low, spreading branches surrounded by younger trees with branch-free lower stems tells the tracker that the area was an open field in the youth of the larger tree. That plant had plenty of light on all sides, and so did not shed its lower branches. The other trees grew up later, shading one another and dropping their shaded, useless lower branches as their crowns raced and crowded into the light. A tree's life thus becomes a slow dance, with light and shade calling the dance steps. Consideration of the tree's species in relation to the soil and successional processes, various forms of scarring from lightning, frost and mechanical damage, and other clues allow an even more detailed reconstruction of the life of a tree and the landscape around it.

The shape of the surface of the ground is the largest track, and covers the longest span of time. Here the tracks are signs of geological forces, and can be enormous. Continental glaciers shaped the Great Lakes region, and their tracks cover several states and provinces. Such features as moraines, kames, kettles and dunes tell of the glacial progress, retreat and aftermath.

We are part of the landscape, and several people have noted how tracking inevitably leads us back to ourselves. First, Tom Brown, Jr. (1978, p. 1), who draws from a Native American perspective: "The tracks of every mystery you have ever swallowed move inside your own tracks, shading them slightly or skewing them with nuances that show how much *more* you have become than what you were." Here is an observation on the indigenous Australians (Allen 1975, p. 2): "To these people, an emu's print is truly more than a bird's track; it is the bird itself and also its spirit and their totemic ancestor, and this is not all. The three-toed footprint conveys to them a sense of song, dance and ceremony." Finally, an Asian perspective as passed on by Joseph Campbell (1986, p. 31-32): "In India, ...as noticed by Ananda K. Coomaraswamy, works of art...representing deities or revered ancestors, such as might appear in temples or on domestic shrines, are perceived as tokens of an inward, spiritual 'way' or 'path,' termed *marga*, which is a word derived from the vocabulary of the hunt, denoting the tracks or trail of an animal, by following which the hunter comes to his quarry." I wish you good hunting, to whatever degree you choose to develop your tracking sense in particular, and your awareness in general.

The following story, another of my Alaska experiences, touches on tracking and awareness in several ways.

The Edge

When I woke up, I found myself in my little pack tent. I was miles from the base camp. I had walked out close to the Bering Sea to collect some gulls as part of my graduate research in wildlife biology. I moved, and every muscle was sore. It was the height of the spring thaw, and the lowland tundra was a flat, slushy landscape. I had exhausted myself the previous day wading through deep, melting snow in hip boots with snowshoes strapped over the feet. That had worked fine until a snowshoe knifed in sideways, dumping me into the slush. It was only knee deep, but with the fatigue, the tangled snowshoes, and the pack weighing me down it took a long ten seconds for me to stand. That was enough time for the boots to fill with ice water. I had struggled to this little dry island, one of the round-topped hills the Yupiks call pingos, set up camp, and slept for nine hours. Now I wanted to get back to base camp.

I unzipped the door of the tent for a look outside. Snow was falling. Snow, in mid-May. The falling snow gave me mixed feelings. It increased the hardship fractionally, but it also brought back feelings of Christmas time. I could hear "Jingle Bells" playing in my head. There was half an inch of accumulation. It was falling so thickly that I couldn't see very far. I was looking at a landscape without edges. I couldn't see the Askinuk Mountains to the north. Turning south, I couldn't see the bluffs, either. The bluffs formed the hard, elevated route I would follow most of the way back to base camp. But I couldn't follow what I couldn't see. I closed the tent door and slept for another hour.

By then the snow had changed to a misty Bering Sea rain. Visibility was better. I could see the snow-covered sides of the bluffs, a sinuous white line against the gray sky, more than a mile to the south. I ate some dried fruit, heated a cup of tea on the little camp stove, and dressed, wincing as I pulled on the cold, wet hip boots.

I packed everything except the rifle. I felt I should make a token effort to collect a gull or two. I wanted to find what they were eating, and to take measurements and specimens from them. Then I would take the meat back to camp and find some way to cook it, as my family ethic dictated. I felt I should eat anything I shoot. The day before I had failed to get a sitting shot. Now a glaucous gull flew toward me and began to circle overhead. I shot at it, and missed. I shot several more times, but managed only to nick its foot. The bird dangled a leg slightly as it flew away, the edge of its white wing cutting across the dark gray sky. The gull left behind three bright red drops on the snow. They were harsh, a poke in the eye, the only color for miles in a landscape of gray and white and brown. I put away the rifle. The rain stopped.

Now it was a long, hard trudge to the bluffs. I was tired, and sore, and just wanted to get back to the tent frame. In the deep slush I wore hip boots with snowshoes over the feet. I came to a meltwater lake that was too wide to go around. I took off the snow-shoes and waded, carefully because the bottom of the lake was a sheet of slick, white ice. I crossed four such lakes and a mile of slush before I reached the bluffs and climbed up onto the hard, snow-free ground along the up-per edge.

Now the going was better beneath that heavy gray sky. The bluffs would take me within two miles of base camp. The only challenge was provided by gullies which had eroded into the bluffs during the heavier rains of Pleistocene times. They were filled with vegetation in summer, and with wind-packed snow in winter. It was only now, during the thaw, that they drained the upland tundra behind the bluffs, channeling the water into the lowland I had just crossed. Each gully was the channel for a swift meltwater stream, across which I had to step or wade. When I waded I took careful, 4-inch sidesteps and faced into the current, because the streams were ice-bottomed like those meltwater lakes had been. Once I was thirsty and so I knelt, balancing the big pack on my back, and watching the tops of the hip boots as I leaned forward to touch my lips to the icy water in one of the smaller streams.

And once, as I started to climb out of one of the largest gul-lies, a tundra hare got up and ran ahead of me. I had never seen a tundra hare. It was huge, and so graceful as it loped up the hill. It was eerie, too, its winter coat a shade grayer than the white snow. It had no shadow, the clouds were too thick. The ghostlike hare stopped at the top of the gully, stood on its hind feet and looked back at me. I moved slightly. The hare vanished. When I reached the top I could see for miles, but I could not see the hare.

After hours of hiking in this way, I reached the point where the line of bluffs came closest to the base camp. I could see the tent frame, a cream-colored rectangle on a large pingo in the lowland tundra two miles north. It always looked strange, that rectangle, square corners and straight lines in a landscape of round forms and curved lines. It looked strange, but it was where I wanted to be.

Here the bluff had risen fifty feet above the lowland tundra. As I stepped up to the snowy rim, ready to climb down the curved slope, I ... stopped. I looked at the ground in front of me. Something bothered me, bothered me enough to delay my return to camp. The snowy sides of the bluffs were like an apron which blended with the slush of the lowlands below me. I stared and stared at that apron of snow. Then, gradually, a line came into view, across my path about two feet in front of my toes. It was the faintest of lines in the snow. It was as though someone had taken a sheet of paper, painted half of it with white paint, then mixed a single drop of black with the rest of the white paint and covered the other half of the paper. The line was the boundary between those two halves. The snow was clean. There was no shadow. As I continued to stare, I realized what the line was. The wind had packed the snow into a thirty-foot vertical cliff. The line was the top edge of that cliff. If I had taken one more step, I would have gone over. I see myself doing a slow, surprised half-flip, then my neck snapping as the heavy pack jolts against it at the bottom of the bluff.

Shaking with more than fatigue, I climbed down at another spot and made the weary home stretch through the slush to camp. But I had had an experience. I had gained a metaphor which remains with me to this day. For I had come to the edge of death, and I had found it to be not the difference between light and darkness, but rather a step between barely discernable shadings of light.

Chapter 10: Program Design

In the last session on the last day of the 1995 National Association for Interpretation national workshop in Orlando, I went to a presentation entitled "Compelling Stories---Compellingly Told," by a National Park Service administrator named Connie Rudd. I was blitzed by then, having gone to many presentations. People often skip the final afternoon entirely, and so I was surprised to find the room nearly full. There was a sense of anticipation. I soon realized that most of the crowd were themselves NPS interpreters. My impression was that Rudd's presentation was good, and the materials she distributed were reasonably innovative, but not enough at first glance to justify the crowd's enthusiasm. Clearly there was something happening in the NPS, but just what it was I couldn't say. At that point I didn't have the energy to pursue the question.

I got a more complete picture at the 1996 national workshop in Billings, thanks to a series of six presentations by the quartet of Dave Dahlen, David Larsen, Sandy Weber and Robert Fudge. I attended two of those talks, and now appreciate that there really is something innovative emerging. Their approach is close to the heart of what I have been calling Deep Interpretation.

The NPS framework is complex enough that I won't pretend to comprehend it from what I've seen so far. One central process brings out connections between the interpretive site or other object of interpretation and meaningful, universal values we human beings share. Stories are developed that point to these connections in compelling ways.

David Larsen held up an antique firearm (actually he didn't, because of aviation security concerns about his transporting it---a hijacking with a nonfunctional model of an antique weapon would

151

be a compelling story itself). Start over: David Larsen *pretended* to hold up an antique firearm, and soon was painting the picture of a hearthside chat between a father and son, both of whom had made firearms with the same manufacturer at Harper's Ferry. The father had worked there when everything was done by hand. The son was now working under conditions of mass production. Their hypothetical discussion brought out both the tangible features of these different processes (individualized products of craftsmanship vs. the consistent products of the industrial revolution, for instance) and intangible meanings of these features (with mass production came a loss of pride in the full investment of self into the production of a complete product; at the same time, there was a gain in material wealth and security for the worker).

Larsen's theme in this model presentation had to do with how the transition from craft to manufacturing impacted the world views of the workers. But more important was his desire to bring out intangible meanings while talking about more tangible objects, processes and concepts. Larsen wants people to care about the material he interprets, making it relevant to them by tying his story to universal values or concepts such as family, community, freedom, power, love, work, beauty, joy, God, etc.: i.e., larger and more powerful intangibles. More specifically, the method Larsen outlined is to take an object or site and make a list of significant meanings. Why did people preserve this site or object? What impact has it had on the lives of people who touched it? These meanings become links in the sequential points made in an interpretive presentation, alternating with tangible elements and building toward some expression of the universal(s). As in any good story, the intangibles are brought out indirectly. "Show, don't tell," is a fiction writer's applicable credo.

David Larsen's presentation was brilliant and powerful. The same holds for Robert Fudge's talk toward the end of the conference. Fudge portrayed a Professor of Interpretation, a character which allowed him to have a lot of fun with his audience while describing some of his group's ideas in a more theoretical way. He described an "interpretive equation:" the sum of one's knowledge of the resource and knowledge of the audience, when multiplied by the appropriate techniques, equals or produces an interpretive opportunity (not interpretation per se, which in Fudge's view takes place in the minds and hearts of the audience). The ultimate goal is to guide the audience to care for the resource. The interpreter reveals relevant meanings through carefully selected and developed stories. The interpreter seeks to create a curiosity and interest within the audience members which will lead them to reflect upon the site, find their own understanding and appreciation of it, and ultimately support its stewardship or preservation.

This new NPS model has influenced my thinking in program design. I have begun to experiment with mini-programs for Willowbrook's casual visitors, following my understanding of NPS practices, but these are new enough at this writing that I don't know, yet, how they will work out. Of course, too rigid a program structure is not desirable, and there are circumstances when structure is to be avoided, as the following story perhaps illustrates.

The Roger Raccoon Club Campout

I watched a brief TV debate on a network news program, the morning before the Fourth of July, 1998, regarding a proposed constitutional amendment prohibiting the burning of an American flag. On one side was a one-time prisoner of war who spoke passionately in support of peoples' right to make statements of protest, even if frowned upon by the majority, and including the freedom to burn a flag, as long as the flag belongs to the protester. The ex-P.O.W.'s opponent maintained that burning the American flag was an intolerable desecration. That issue has fascinated me for a long time.

When I was growing up, the word most commonly associated with the American flag was freedom. Abstractions and metaphors can be difficult for a child to grasp. When I was small, teachers frequently used the phrase that our ancestors "were of British soil." I took this literally, seeing stacks of people buried beneath the ground. However, it was clear enough to me that the flag was not freedom. The flag was an object that represented freedom. But in this debate we see a rare kind of conflict, a conflict between a symbol on one side and what that symbol represents on the other. Which do we value more highly, freedom or the flag? There are many people who are eager to sacrifice certain freedoms to protect the American flag. This seems ironic, that we might compromise what the flag represents while keeping the flag itself. But the issue is more subtle than that. It's not simply the flag, but the feelings of people regarding it, that are damaged when the flag is burned. And, as Etzioni (1996) points out, freedom is only half of the equation. A "voluntary moral order" is needed, and some might argue that protecting the flag is a necessary part of that order. So, like so many debates in our society, this one resolves fuzzily: deeply hurt feelings on one side, freedom of expression on the other. We Americans value our individuality, our rights and our freedoms, but temper them by setting up laws which say those rights and freedoms do not mean you can freely hurt others, killing or injuring them or stealing their property.

This TV debate took place the morning after one of our Roger Raccoon Club campouts. The Roger Raccoon Club is a program we offer to 9-12-year-olds. They come to my center for 7 hours on Monday, 7 hours on Tuesday, then we go to another forest preserve for an overnight campout, from 9 am on Wednesday to 9 am on Thursday. Although we focus on learning activities and natural history explorations on Monday and Tuesday, I build a lot of looseness into the campout. During that 24-hour period we have some games and activities, but also a lot of free time. The children are not permitted to bring radios, computer games, or other electronic devices, so they are put in a position where they must organize their own time. They make up their own games, their own rules. They do things which sometimes I would rather they not do---using language I'd rather not hear, or attempting feats of daring (climbing trees, for instance) which could lead, potentially, to injury. Sometimes I intervene. When words are used that hurt others' feelings, I stop the play and point this out. When a child is at-

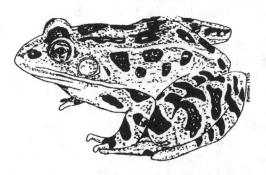

tempting to climb a tree that others are climbing but is beyond that child's ability, I stop the child but spare feelings by saying that the tree has as many people in it as I can allow. The child usually understands, and is even grateful to have been released from a fear-evoking activity.

It was only after hearing the flag-burning debate that I realized how fundamentally American is my style with the Roger Raccoon Club. On the one hand we give them plenty of exposure to the out-of-doors, and to topics of natural history. But, more than many programs, we also turn them loose. The 9-12 age range is at the threshold of adult experience. They can and, I believe should, be given some responsibility and the freedom to make choices. But that freedom has to be tempered with protection. I cannot allow some kids to be hurt by the free expressions of others. At the same time, I feel it appropriate and needful to point out why I am intervening when I do so. I try to be clear not only about the harmful nature of certain words and acts, but also about choice and responsibility. They can choose to think about what they say to others, and they also can choose how to respond to what others are saying to them. I am attempting to reinforce two community enhancing values that Etzioni (1996) recommends educators transmit to children: empathy, and the ability to control impulses. The balance of freedom against protection---it's a fundamentally American concept.

The tents were set, and the kids very quickly completed the morning's organized activities, lessons in ecosystem ecology to complement the previous two days' focus on natural history of various plants and animals. This group of kids had given us some discipline problems over the previous two days, but paradoxically they were eager participants in learning activities. While my seasonal assistants and I set up for lunch, I gave the kids the assignment to find examples of leaf miners around the periphery of our campsite. Later, after they had roasted their turkey franks over the campfire and sampled other lunch foods, we hiked down to the "waterfall," where a small creek poured over an old sawmill dam. The kids loved the creek, tiptoeing from rock to rock, tentatively walking across the dam, finally wading in the pool below the dam. Inevitably some fell in. They enjoyed splashing, finding crayfish, climbing the dam, getting a firsthand experience of the stream as it interpreted itself. I was alert for hazards, but ended up saying nothing as the kids were being careful, taking only small risks.

We walked along a wooded trail above the creek, then. I became aware of sounds of crying. I turned around to find 9-year-old Amy in tears. Jean, 11, had an arm around Amy's shoulders. I knelt down: "What's wrong, Amy?" She sobbed, "I heard Emily tell Richard that he should say he doesn't like me." Emily, just turned 11, had proven to be the Roger Raccoon Club's femme fatale, a rare phenomenon in the club's history. After toying with the hearts of a couple of the other boys, she focused on 9-year-old Richard, with whom Amy was enjoying a new friendship. The seasonals, Jean and I comforted her with assurances of her value, and I emphasized that Emily, Richard and Amy all had choices to make, both in their own actions and in their responses to the actions of others. Amy was somewhat mollified, and we continued, me pointing out animals, plants and other items of interest. Jean stayed with Amy. She began proselytizing, repeating a rotememorized statement about being Saved, the comforts therein, and the unhappy consequences of failing to do so. I was not entirely comfortable about this, but gut feeling said not to intrude. I focused on Jean's words, her tone of voice. She was genuinely concerned for Amy's feelings. After her presentation, Amy politely said, "I don't know, I'll have to think about it." I heard nothing more along this line the rest of the campout. Within half an hour of our return to camp, Amy, Emily and Richard all were laughing together. I just shook my head, amazed at the emotional volatility of people at that age.

A Project WILD activity was followed by dinner, cooked over the campfire, then a night hike and campfire stories. Then ensued a struggle to get the kids to sleep as post-midnight taunts and challenges flew back and forth between the largest boys' tent and the largest girls' tent. After my repeated demands for quiet were ignored, I ordered the 5 principals in this exchange out of their tents, told them we were going on another night hike, required them to leave their flashlights on one of the picnic tables, and we set out. I stopped them after 100 yards. They were subdued. I gave them the choice of sleeping or continuing the hike. They opted for sleep, and the rest of the night was quiet. Here, teaching them to control impulses, and protecting the sleep of those who wished to do so, were my guiding principles. I admit that this "moral order" was not entirely "voluntary."

The next morning Allen, 9, who had been very interested in the fire but had been unsafe with it, requiring me to restrict his activity around it, packed early and was ready to be picked up by his father. The other kids were dawdling over breakfast and the packing process. I taught Allen how to gather small, dry dead twigs from standing trees and use them to restart the fire from last night's remaining coals. I coached him, but otherwise didn't help. It took him a while, and he almost gave up twice, but ultimately the flames burst forth, and we all cheered, his own cries sharp and triumphant. Soon the parents arrived, and after a few diplomatic words and good-byes, it was all done: another campout in America.

Chapter 11: The Power of Words

Importance of Words

There are underlying layers of communication in any interaction, and this is at least as true in interpretation as in any other form. Even our choice of words leads to unintended messages. The meanings of words are not always straightforward, and in particular there are certain terms that trouble me. They are good illustrations of how a word can have meanings at more than one level, communicating assumptions and messages of which we are unaware.

For instance, the words "environment" and "nature," as they commonly are used, teach that human beings are separable from the Earth, when the intention often is the opposite. These words are names, nouns, which automatically convert the concepts to which they refer into isolated objects. There's the environment or nature over there, here are the people over here. But if the reality is that people are a part of nature, how can there be anything that is not natural? How can the word "environment" have meaning when it is impossible for a person to be separate from an environment and survive for more than a few pain-wracked moments of suffocation? Such words are abstractions without reality, but our use of them gives them an apparent reality which contradicts our purpose as interpreters. I try to avoid these words, for instance substituting "wild" for "natural" in many usages.

"Wilderness" is another tough word. I believe that the word "wilderness" is entirely arbitrary in its definition. Some peoples' definitions can get technical, hinging on the absence of mechanical contrivances. To others, the idea of wilderness requires the absence of people entirely. It all seems artificial and suspect to me. At least from the time of the glacier to the present day, human beings have occupied and impacted every landscape on the continent. We're talking about a 10,000-year span of time. I've already revealed my bias that there are no people apart from nature. I'm inclined to believe also that there is no nature without us. The trick is to avoid impacting wild places to the extent that populations are lost or fundamental ecological processes are poisoned or derailed. There also is value in having places where a person can go, escaping the influence of other people to view himself or herself in the pure mirror of a wild place.

"Earth Day"

Now: does the celebration of "Earth Day" teach that one day is enough? How general is the attitude reflected in the comment of one child, overheard to say while leaving an Earth Day event, "Well, we've saved the Earth. We can go home now." I am concerned that the name and structure of the event itself communicate this message, contradicting anything said to the contrary during the event. In other words, I feel that the notion of "Earth Day" communicates that its issues can be dealt with in a day, and therefore can be dismissed when that day is done. Keep in mind also that those who don't attend but only hear about Earth Day are being taught, too, by the name alone. The more we highlight Earth Day events, the more we imply to the non-attending public that these issues are of negligible importance.

I recently dug out of my closet an old gray pocket folder with "1970 Environmental Teach-In" on its cover. It's so old I can still read my handwriting, which was much clearer in those days. Names and telephone numbers of Purdue's first Earth Day committee are written there as well, but inside the folder are mainly the handwritten manuscripts for the series of columns I was writing for Purdue's student newspaper a couple of years after the Teach-In. By then, Earth Day was regarded as an event of historical significance, but there was work to be done. And today I feel that while such language as "Environmental Teach-In" is dated, something like it would avoid limiting the significance of the event to a single day out of the year. Granted, there is name recognition in Earth Day, and a nostalgic value. Perhaps some sort of transition in name and consciousness (my own Forest Preserve District put on a large event, calling it "Earth Day's Birthday," which falls in this category), or an elaboration of the name (e.g., "Earth Education

Day") would have not only the benefit of escaping a weak name, but also would demonstrate the continuing importance of Earth community and human survival issues.

Something else that may be going on with Earth Day and other special events is a desire to re-create the old rituals and ceremonies that honor the seasons, rites of passage, and so forth. Earth Day events, Arbor Day events, May Day, the Kentucky Derby, all celebrate the spring, the resurgence of life and vitality. Our quest for ritual in a community context, painfully lacking in our society, needs to be addressed, but consciously rather than indirectly.

Defining "Interpretation"

I would like to conclude this chapter by addressing the definition of "interpretation" itself (as an interpretive naturalist, I write about my segment of the interpretive field; I am sure that cultural and historical interpreters can translate my ideas into terms suitable for their work). Suppose that every person on our continent were an Aldo Leopold, a Rachel Carson or a John Muir. These people achieved a powerful sense of connectedness with the Earth, and because they realized that their vision was both rare and desperately needed by society, they acted to spread it to others. If every person shared their understanding, we quickly would work to resolve the problems we are creating for the Earth and for our own survival prospects. The political-pressure and monkey-wrench tactics would become obsolete.

Is it too idealistic to expect that a sense of oneness with the Earth would pervade a culture? In fact there are precedents on this continent. The traditional components of most Native American societies understand their dependence upon the Earth, with a sense of attachment and participation in natural processes that has deep roots.

It has become a cliche that Native Americans were the first ecologists. In recent years reactionaries have pointed out cases of ecological disharmony among ancient Native Americans in the form of excessive killings of large animals, occasional massacres in warfare, and the like. But this does not take away Native Americans' basic love of the Earth. It simply demonstrates that indigenous people are human beings, capable of making mistakes, endowed with their fair share of capacity for evil, and displaying a broad range of stereotype-stifling individuality. I fully expect that if the truth were known, the Native American hunter's renowned re-

161

spect for his prey would trace directly back to the Pleistocene overkill. Mistakes are tremendous teachers, and such a colossal error could teach a stable society lessons that would last a long time. Native Americans have lived in this part of the world a minimum of twelve thousand years. There is space in that time span for many major mistakes. The result of that long painful learning process was a group of societies in which people, both as individuals and in concert, take the welfare of their grandchildren into account when making even small decisions.

So indigenous Americans possess the sense of oneness with the Earth that Leopold, Carson and Muir discovered, and it permeated their societies. How do they transmit it to their children? If all interpreters knew and emulated the techniques that allow generation after generation of traditionally oriented Native Americans to pass on their love of the Earth, we could help our society move toward the goal I have stated.

I summarize the central idea in a definition: Nature Interpretation---teaching people to hear and understand the language of the Earth.

People who are connected with the Earth treat her as a living being, even if their intellect regards this understanding as a sort of internal metaphor. We naturalists have been touched by the voice of the Earth, as were Leopold and Carson and Muir. It is that contact which motivates us---high salaries or power certainly do not draw people to our profession, and intellectual curiosity is not sufficient. Nor does effective interpretation in itself bring people to the Earth. My own interest in nature began when adult friends performed casual interpretation for me, but my commitment grew out of my own subjective experiences of being touched by the Earth. Think about it. Isn't your own professional choice the result of your solitary experiences in contact with the land?

Most definitions of nature interpretation emphasize the teaching techniques interpreters use, creating confusion, because when most people are confronted with the word "interpretation" they think of language translation. I prefer to say that I am a person who interprets the language of the Earth and helps other people learn to do so as well.

Accepting this definition requires some humility. It regards interpreters as middlemen leading people to the final step. The Earth completes the process, interpreting herself in voices which speak a little differently to each person.

No one raised in a European-derived society is going to make a sudden leap from indifference about nature to oneness with the Earth. If we begin by sharing our deepest feelings and understandings, no matter how subtle our technique, we will turn most people away. We need to gain their trust, become familiar to them, dealing at first with the more straightforward and simple languages of the Earth before moving to the more advanced. We need to move up the pyramid Maslow drew, resolving fears and other basic issues before understanding can be fostered.

Science is characterized by objectivity---it deals with phenomena that are repeatable and observable by most people using the conventional senses of vision, hearing, touch, etc. This makes scientific understanding relatively easy to communicate. But the best

science can do is make nature interesting to people. Science will not help people to love or care for the Earth. Science appeals to the intellect, and the intellect ingeniously maneuvers to avoid acknowledging problems. Countless studies of acid rain, ozone-layer erosion, and the relationship between deforestation and famine have been made, and still people demand more studies before they will act.

Nevertheless, interpretation of the Earth's function in scientific terms remains an essential step, informing people of their participation in natural processes and their dependence upon the Earth. Interpretation that makes use of science plants cognitive seeds which more advanced interpretation, based on aesthetics and higher values, will nurture. If the interpreter is to facilitate this process, much depends on the interpreter's commitment and personal depth of understanding. It is important for the interpreter to develop his or her own centeredness and sense of connection with the Earth.

Nature interpretation is teaching people to hear and understand the languages of the Earth. But an interpretive naturalist is a healer---someone who lovingly salves and binds the conceptual and spiritual wounds separating people from their Earth Mother.

The overall theme of this chapter has been that language can entrap us. Here is a transcultural story on that theme, my retelling based on Shah (1966) and Serwer (1970).

If Copper Can Die

A wise fool was holding a feast, and so he borrowed a set of pots from his neighbor. After the feast he returned the pots, along with an extra one, a little tiny pot.

The neighbor said, "I cannot accept this pot. It is not one that I loaned you. I am no thief."

But the fool said, "While your pots were in my care, they gave birth. This little pot is their baby, and it is yours by law." The neighbor was pleased at this, and accepted the little pot without further questions.

A couple of months later, the fool held another feast, and again he borrowed the pots. The neighbor gave them up willingly, thinking that in the bountiful house of the fool they would again bring forth. This time, though, several days passed, and the pots had not been returned. The neighbor came to the fool. "Where are my pots?"

"Oh, I am sorry to have to tell you. They died. It was a lovely funeral."

"Died? What do you mean? Copper cannot die."

"Did we not establish that your pots gave birth? And is it not true that anything that brings forth is mortal?"

The fool kept the pots.

Chapter 12: Modeling

A father didn't really teach his sons; his life threw lessons in the air like scraps to gulls, and different mouths latched onto different morsels. (Laurence Shames 1995, *Sunburn* [novel])

There are no casual acts. Each thing we do is like a seed put into the fist of God. As that hand opens in the fullness of time, the seed sprouts and flourishes and becomes a tree that casts thousands of its own seed over all the future, changing things in little and big ways. (Nancy N. Baxter 1987, The Movers [novel])

Significance of Modeling

What is the most fundamental teaching method, in your view? To me the answer seems very clear: it's modeling. Through the example of our lives, in our behavior as witnessed by others, we are teaching almost constantly. This is true of everyone, interpreters or not, whether we are engaged in interpretive actions or not: all of us are providing lessons in ways to be.

Two of the most impressive interpreters I have ever seen in action were volunteers, one at Big Basin Redwoods State Park in California, the other at Mesa Verde National Park in Colorado. Monica, the California interpreter, regards redwood trees with a consuming passion that she expressed in every word and gesture, as she led a field trip group at the NAI National Workshop in 1992. She has absorbed every word ever written about redwoods, both in the popular and technical press. She has studied the history of redwood conservation. She has spent days in the presence of those big trees. She talks with everyone who will listen, sharing the story of the redwoods' wonderful resilience, their remarkable

167

strategies for achieving longevity. There is a persistent quality in their lives which Monica shares, and the strength of her feeling spreads to those for whom she interprets.

I was weakened by a virus when visiting Mesa Verde, and so failed to note the name of the woman from Texas who was interpreting one of the ruins there as she has, all summer, for many years. Like Monica, this volunteer has an enthusiasm that permeates her being. She has learned everything she can about her subject, and her fascination is contagious. She told stories of talking with visiting Hopi and Acoma people, and they trusted her enough to share some of what they knew about the "Anasazi," builders of the Mesa Verde cliff dwellings, their ancestors. Such openness, I am sure, was a response to her honest love of the place and its past, without any of the ulterior motives that might be attributed to an archeologist, anthropologist, or staff ranger.

I doubt that many could resist being taken in by the passion these two women hold for their subjects. It's much more than their words. They provide the best examples I have encountered of the power of modeling in interpretation.

Modeling can be more specific and mundane, as well. The respect one shows when approaching an animal, plant or artifact; being courteous and graceful when asked a challenging or even hatred-based question; being willing to admit ignorance, or awe, or that one has made a mistake: all of these are examples of modeling.

Nonverbal Communication

What is all this about? The idea of modeling certainly is not one of the first things one thinks about when considering interpretive technique. Yet there is a very good reason for giving this element of interpretation greater attention. Modeling is a form of nonverbal communication. Nonverbal communication includes gestures and other forms of body language, as well as variables of speech other than words, for example the changes in emphasis brought about by varying volume, pitch, etc. In a sense, modeling is a synonym for nonverbal communication in a teaching-learning context. You probably have heard those statistics commonly spouted in the popular press or in lectures about communication, that 60 or 75 or 90 percent of communication is nonverbal. The words we use are, according to these statistics, relatively unimportant. Usually such statistics are stated without much exploration of their implications. But think of what this means. If we want to be effective interpreters, we should be spending a lot more time studying nonverbal communication, understanding its significance, than we do.

Before I felt I could write anything more on this subject, I decided I had better see what scholars of communication had to say about it. Where do these statistics come from, anyway? I found a recent review of nonverbal communication (Burgoon 1994), and learned that actually there has been very little research on the importance of nonverbal communication. The oft-quoted numbers are derived indirectly. Sometimes they simply are estimates by people who have studied the subject for many years. Some studies have looked at how much of the variance in meaning in communicative transactions can be attributed to the words in the message (31%, on average). "The remainder presumably [is] accounted for by nonverbal cues or their interaction with verbal ones" (Burgoon, p. 235). In other words, most statistics on the importance of nonverbal communication are reached through a process of elimination rather than a direct demonstration. There is so little study of this subject that any conclusions need to be regarded as tentative. Nevertheless, I am influenced by studies demonstrating that when there is a conflict between the words someone is saying and the nonverbal cues that person is broadcasting, people reject the words and trust the body language, vocal inflections, pauses, pitch, loudness, etc. This suggests that nonverbal cues are regarded as more important than words, are trusted more, and thus constitute more than half of what is communicated.

So, why not just fool 'em? Learn about body language, and control it? Practice speaking so the voice always projects a truthful impression, whether you believe what you're saying or not, whether you know your subject or not? I doubt that this is possible. For one thing, we don't really know enough about how this nonverbal stuff works. Studies of deceptive behavior have not established how successful people can be at lying. People who study deception have concluded that facial expression is the least reliable deception clue, and the voice is the greatest channel carrying cues to deception. But even these conclusions are really the researchers' educated guesses, not yet backed by data.

There are many difficult subtleties in nonverbal communication that might lead to pitfalls. One example that I think about often is the handling of live wild animals in interpretive programming. The image of a person holding a snake, raptor, bat, taran-tula, etc., is powerful. Lots of people, including myself and others at my center, use such techniques. Audiences are responsive to such programming, and people often come away with distinct, positive impressions and lessons. Yet I can't help but wonder if the image of a person holding a wild animal is subtly teaching (through the powerful, nonverbal method of modeling) that wild animals, and by extension wild places, are subordinate to human beings. If people are the masters of the Earth, then a hawk on a leash is a clear emblem of that superior, controlling status. But is this an idea we really want to reinforce? So far, I feel that the snakes I save from being hacked in half with hoes because people have learned to be sympathetic with one they have touched in my hands are more important than my unproven concerns about sub-tle meta-messages. But I still worry about it.

Another subtle aspect of modeling is the fact that there are symbolic qualities in the way we see and are seen. The interpreter is not just another human being, but also is Man or Woman, Teacher, Ranger, etc., and any modeling we do is, I believe, per-ceived in part through the lens of these ideals.

But even with the power of such symbols behind us, in the end I don't think it's possible to be deceptive. And even if it is, it wouldn't be worth the effort. There are too many gestures, too many subtle vocal tensions and inflections to control. I conclude that the better solution for me is to decide how I want to be and then polish my life so as to be it as honestly as I can. The phe-nomenon of modeling will take care of the rest, automatically.

Seed Planting

Interpreters are at one great disadvantage with respect to classroom teachers. We do not have the luxury of working with the same students for an extended period of time. Any teaching we do, any role modeling we perform, is just a touch. We will be anonymous in our visitors' memories, certainly as compared to those classroom teachers whose names will remain with them into adulthood. They will retain the story of their time with us, and it is up to us to make sure that story is a good one. But realistically, our influence is small in terms of the time they spend with us relative to their other activities. Most of the people we contact will spend more time in front of the TV on that day. We all realize this, and it's tempting to be depressed by it.

But a holistic view can help, here. Our egos want us to be the most important influence any of our visitors will ever have in their entire lives. But we are individually only small parts of a huge Earth. Each contact we make is part of a sequence of influences that will affect our constituent's relationship with the Earth. Commonly that person will have encountered others before us, and certainly there will be others after us. We are planters of seeds. We plant words, actions and artifacts in the experience of the people we contact, and the kinds of seeds we plant make a difference. We need to make sure the seeds are good ones. But we also need to remember that they won't be the only ones. The best ones are those the person finds in the Earth in a moment of discovery that mirrors back Self-recognition. That process, which goes on whether we acknowledge it or not, frees us to give them the best seeds we can, the ones that best reflect our particular love for the Earth. And sometimes, the impact of a seed is amazingly disproportionate. The vast majority of the thousands of seeds released by a large cottonwood tree fail to grow to reproductive age. But consider the tiny, almost weightless cottonwood seed and the massive tree into which it will grow if successful. We have no way of knowing at the time which of our interpretive moments, exhibit details or unconscious bits of modeling will influence someone disproportionately. But some of them do.

Examples of seeds: a frown. A smile. A spider web glinting with jewels of dew. A freshly opened flower. A moment's glance that connects you with a person, lets him or her know you acknowledge their value. The image of you in a uniform, addressing the group in a friendly and confident manner. A robin, its beak stuffed with earthworms. A well told story. An ecological process shown to be beautiful by your interpretation of it. A coyote scat full of rabbit hair. The uniqueness of a leaf.

"Have a good life" was a poignant expression that became cliched by overuse a few years ago. It represents an interpreter's attitude in more ways than one, however. We want our visitors to be happy in the wake of their visit to us, and our well-wishing is part of our healthy attitude toward them, as we expect never to see them again. At the same time, we regard our work as important, and the lessons that come from our sites and missions do contribute to the making of good lives, if heeded and taken to heart.

The relationship between behavioral or role modeling and seed planting is plain to me. I believe that our modeling is made most effective when we fully respect the people for whom we are interpreting. Some tricks for respecting others:

1. Remember that in each person you are impacting an entire life: within the adult you are addressing there is a child that lives on, observing and remembering and subconsciously commenting. The child before you will carry the memory of your time together into adulthood.

2. See the person purely, without judgement or label or category or assumption, and accept the accompanying impressions of beauty and love.

3. Study learning styles and related topics until the validity and value of each different manner of being is thoroughly impressed into your consciousness.

4. I'm not a big believer in reincarnation, but I've had fun with the thought that there is only one person---you---in the Universe, going through every life that ever was, is, or will be, passing back and forth through time to do so (this thought also gives additional depth to the Golden Rule).

Have a good life.

Chickadee Song

By Carl Strang © 1993

Gm

1.If you're walk-in' through the for-est and you
2.I   eat   lit - tle in - sects that I
3.The   for-est   is my gym - nas - tic
4.There are things   you can learn   from

D7   Gm

hap-pen to see   an   up-side down, ac - ro - ba -tic
find in   trees,and I watch out for hawks that would like
ap -pa -rat- us,and   my fam- ly and me, we like to
watch -in' us birds. You can learn by im - i -ta -tion,you

D7   Gm

chick- a - dee,   pay   at - ten - tion and
to   eat   me.   Win - ter/or sum - mer, it's
make   a   fuss.   You   can hear/us singin' all
don't need words.   You   can have/fun/with - out

F   D7   Gm   F   D7   Gm Chorus

you may find that hav-in' a good time's a state of mind. Chick-a
all the same.   Life to me   is one fast paced game.
through the day,   hav- in' fun   the   chickadee way.
be -ing rude, just keep a chick - a -dee at - ti - tude.

- dee - dee - dee,   chick -a - dee-dee- dee,   chick -a

Gm   F   D7   Gm

dee - dee - dee,   life is one big game to me.

173

Literature Cited

Acker, T.S., and A.M. Muscat. 1976. The ecology of *Craspeda custa sowerbii* Lankester, a freshwater hydrozoan. *Am. Midl. Nat.* 95:323-336.

Allen, Louis A. 1975. *Time before morning*. Thomas Y. Crowell Co., N.Y.

Armstrong, Edward A. 1973. *Saint Francis: nature mystic*. Univ. of Calif. Press, Berkeley.

Backstein, Karen. 1992. *The blind men and the elephant*. Scholastic, N.Y.

Barber, H.S. 1951. North American fireflies of the genus *Photuris*. *Smithsonian Misc. Collections* 117(1):1-58.

Barton, D., P. Hicks and J. Washburn. 1992. Making connections: creating multi-cultural environmental education programs. Pp. 220-223 in Covel, J., ed. *Proceedings 1992 National Interpreters Workshop*. NAI, Fort Collins.

Basso, Keith H. 1986. Stalking with stories: names, places, and moral narratives among the western Apaches. Pp. 95-116 in Halpern, Daniel, ed.*On Nature: nature, landscape, and natural history*. North Point Press, San Francisco.

Baylor, Byrd. 1986. *I'm in charge of celebrations*. Charles Scribner's Sons, New York.

Best, Elsdon. 1925. *Tuhoe, the children of the mist*. Vol. 1. Thomas Avery & Sons Limited, New Plymouth, New Zealand.

Bettleheim, Bruno. 1976. *The uses of enchantment: the meaning and importance of fairy tales*. Alfred Knopf, New York.

Bierzychudek, Paulette. 1982. The demography of Jack-in-the-pulpit, a forest perennial that changes sex. *Ecol. Monogr.* 52:335-351.

Bradshaw, John. 1990. *Homecoming: reclaiming and championing your inner child.* Bantam, New York.

Brown, Tom, Jr. 1978. *The tracker.* Berkley Books, N.Y.

Brown, Tom, Jr. (with Brandt Morgan). 1983. *Tom Brown's field guide to nature observation and tracking.* Berkley Books, N.Y.

Bruchac, Joseph. 1994. *The Great Ball Game: A Muskogee Story Retold by Joseph Bruchac.* Dial Books for Young Readers, N.Y.

Buckley, Thomas. 1979. Doing your thinking. *Parabola* 4(4):29-37.

Burgoon, Judee K. 1994. Nonverbal signals. chapter 7, pp. 229-285 in Knapp, Mark L., and Gerald R. Miller, eds. *Handbook of interpersonal communication.* Second ed. Sage Publications, Thousand Oaks, CA

Butler, K. 1987. *Learning and teaching style in theory and practice.* The Learner's Dimension, Columbia, CT. 317 pp.

Caduto, M., and J. Bruchac. 1988. *Keepers of the Earth.* Fulcrum, Inc., Golden, Colorado.

Campbell, Joseph. 1968. *The hero with a thousand faces.* Bollington Series 17. Princeton Univ. Press, Princeton, NJ.

Campbell, Joseph. 1986. *The inner reaches of outer space.* Harper & Row, New York.

Campbell, Joseph. 1988. *The power of myth, with Bill Moyers.* Doubleday, New York.

Carbo, M., R. Dunn and K. Dunn. 1986. *Teaching students to read through their individual learning styles.* Prentice-Hall, Englewood Cliffs, NJ.

Caskey, O. 1980. *Suggestive-accelerative learning and teaching.* Educational Technology Publications, Englewood Cliffs, NJ.

Chopra, Deepak. 1994. *The seven spiritual laws of success.* Amber-Allen Publishing, San Rafael, California.

Chopra, Deepak. 1995. *The way of the wizard.* Harmony, New York.

Covey, Stephen R. 1989. *The 7 habits of highly effective people.* Simon & Schuster, New York.

Damasio, Antonio R. 1994. *Descarte's error: emotion, reason, and the human brain.* G.P. Putnam's Sons, N.Y.

Davis, Margaret B. 1989. Insights from paleoecology on global change. *Bulletin Ecol. Soc. Am.* 70:222-228.

Dittmer, W. 1907. *Te Tohunga; the ancient legends and traditions of the Maori*. George Routledge and Sons, London.

Estes, Clarissa Pinkola. 1992. *Women who run with the wolves*. Ballantine, New York.

Etzioni, Amitai. 1991a. Too many rights, too few responsibilities. *Society* 28:41-48 (January/February).

Etzioni, Amitai. 1991b. The community in an age of individual ism; an interview with Amitai Etzioni. *The Futurist* 25:35-39 (May-June).

Etzioni, Amitai, ed. 1995. *Rights and the common good*. St. Martin's Press, N.Y.

Etzioni, Amitai. 1996. *The new golden rule*. Basic Books, N.Y.

Fulghum, Robert. 1988. *All I really need to know I learned in kindergarten*. Ivy Books, New York.

Gilmore, Melvin R. 1977. *Uses of plants by the Indians of the Missouri River region*. U. Nebraska Press, Lincoln.

Goleman, Daniel. 1995. *Emotional intelligence*. Bantam Books, N.Y.

Green, John W. 1956. Revision of the nearctic species of *Photinus* (Lampyridae: Coleoptera). *Proc. Calif. Acad. Sci.* 28:561-613.

Green, Julien. 1985. *God's fool; the life and times of Francis of Assissi*. Harper & Row, San Francisco. (Transl. By Peter Heinegg).

Haddock, Randall C., and Stephen J. Chaplin. 1982. Pollination and seed production in two phenologically divergent prairie legumes (*Baptisia leucophaea* and *B. leucantha*). *Am. Midl. Nat.* 108:175-186.

Hallowell, A. 1975. Ojibwa ontology, behavior, and world view. Pp. 141-178 in Tedlock, D., and Tedlock, B, eds. *Teachings from the American earth*. Liveright, New York.

Hardy, Alister. 1979. *The spiritual nature of man: a study of contemporary religious experience*. Clarendon Press, Oxford.

Harrison, Allen F., and Robert M. Bramson. 1982. *The art of thinking*. Berkley Books, NY.

Hess, W.R., and E.v. Holst and U.v.Saint-Paul, as described by Eibl-Eibesfeldt in 1970. *Ethology: the biology of behavior*. New York, N.Y.: Holt, Rinehart and Winston, ch. 9.

Hillman, James. 1979. A note on story. *Parabola* 4(4):43-45.

Hudleston, Dom Roger, translator. 1965. *The little flowers of Saint Francis of Assissi.* The Heritage Press, N.Y.

Johnson, Gerald H., Allan F. Schneider and Herbert P. Ulrich. 1965. *Glacial geology and soils of the area around Lake Maxinkuckee.* Indiana Geological Survey unpublished report.

Jones, Dewitt. 1988. The inner voice. *Outdoor Photographer* 4(8):10.

Keirsey, D., and M. Bates. 1978. *Please understand me.* Prometheus Nemesis Books, Del Mar, CA.

King, Frances B. 1984. Plants, people and paleoecology. *Illinois State Museum Scientific Papers*, Vol. 20.

Kingsbury, J.M. 1964. *Poisonous plants of the United States and Canada.* Prentice-Hall, Englewood Cliffs, N.J.

Lackey, Brenda K. 1997. Electrify your audience. P. 195 *in* Brochu, Lisa, ed. *1997 Interpretive Sourcebook.* National Association for Interpretation.

Lampe, Kenneth F., and Mary Ann McCann. 1985. *AMA handbook of poisonous and injurious plants.* Am. Medical Assoc., Chicago.

Lloyd, James E. 1965. Aggressive mimicry in *Photuris*: firefly femmes fatales. *Science* 149:653-654.

Lloyd, James E. 1980. Male *Photuris* fireflies mimic sexual signals of their females' prey. *Science* 210:669-671.

Loehle, Craig. 1987. Hypothesis testing in ecology: psychological aspects and the importance of theory maturation. *Quart. Rev. Biol.* 62:397-409.

Lopez, Barry. 1978. *Of wolves and men.* Charles Scribner's Sons, N.Y.

Lutz, Ralph H. 1985. Place, home and story in environmental education. *J. Env. Ed.* 16:37-41.

Malone, Thomas Patrick, and Patrick Thomas Malone. 1987. *The art of intimacy.* Prentice Hall, New York.

Maslow, Abraham. 1964. *Religions, values, and peak experiences.* Ohio State University Press, Columbus.

Maslow, Abraham. 1970. *Motivation and personality.* Third Edition. Harper & Row, N.Y.

McCarthy, B. 1987. *The 4MAT system.* Excel, Inc., Barrington, IL.

Meade, Michael. 1993. *Men and the water of life.* HarperCollins, New York.

Mooney, James. 1902. Myths of the Cherokee. Part of *19th Annual Report, Bureau of American Ethnology.* Washington, G.P.O.

Muenscher, W.C. 1975. *Poisonous plants of the United States.* Collier Books, N.Y.

Myers, Isabel Briggs. 1993. Introduction to type. Consulting Psychologists Press, Inc., Palo Alto, California.

Nelson, R. 1983. *Make prayers to the raven: a Koyukon view of the northern forest.* University of Chicago Press.

Opler, Morris E. 1940. *Myths and legends of the Lipan Apache Indians.* Memoirs of the Amer. Folk-lore Soc. Vol. 36: 296 pp.

Paine, R.T., J.T. Watton, and P.D. Boersma. 1990. Direct and indirect effects of peregrine falcon predation on seabird abundance. *Auk* 107:1-9.

Paley, Vivian G. 1990. *The boy who would be a helicopter.* Harvard Univ. Press, Cambridge, MA. 163 pp.

Popper, Karl. 1968. *The logic of scientific discovery.* Harper & Row, N.Y. Quigley, Lillian. 1959. *The blind men and the ele phant.* Charles Scribners Sons, N.Y.

Randi, James. 1980. *Flim-flam! The truth about unicorns, para psychology, and other delusions.* Lippincott & Crowell, N.Y.

Ravich, Diane. 1995. Pluralism within unity: a communitarian version of multiculturalism. Chapter 17, pp. 179-185 *in* Etzioni, Amitai, ed. *Rights and the common good.* St. Martin's Press, N.Y.

Roeder, K.D. 1963. *Nerve cells and insect behavior.* Harvard University Press, Cambridge, Mass.

Rumbaugh, Duane M. 1994. Anthropomorphism revisited. *Q. Rev. Biol.* 69:248-251.

Saxe, John Godfrey. 1963. *The blind men and the elephant.* McGraw-Hill, N.Y.

Serwer, Blanche Luria. 1970. Let's Steal the Moon: Jewish Tales Ancient and Recent. Little, Brown & Co., Boston.

Shah, Idries. 1966. *The exploits of the incomparable Mulla Nasrudin.* Simon & Schuster, N.Y.

Shah, Idries. 1967. *Tales of the Dervishes.* E.P. Dutton, N.Y.

Strang, Carl. 1989a. Advanced awareness techniques. *Proc. 1989 National Interpreters Workshop*:145-147.

Strang, Carl. 1989b. Interpreting the language of the Earth. *J. Interp.* 13:17-20.

Strang, C. 1990. Putting the trees back in the interpretive forest. *Legacy* 1(3):22-24.

Swetnam, Thomas, and Julio Betancourt. 1990. Fire-southern oscillations relations in the southwestern United States. *Science* 249:1017-1020.

Tehanetorens. 1976. *Tales of the Iroquois.* Akwesasne Notes, Mohawk Nation via Rooseveltown, N.Y.

Teit, James A., Livingston Farrand, Marian K. Gould, Herbert J. Spinden. 1917. Folk-tales of Salishan and Sahaptian tribes. *Memoirs of the Am. Folk-lore Soc.* 11:xii+1-205.

Thewissen, J.G.M., S.T. Hussain, and M. Arif. 1994. Fossil evidence for the origin of aquatic locomotion in archaeocete whales. *Science* 263:210-212.

Tilden, Freeman. 1977. *Interpreting our heritage.* Univ. of North Carolina Press, Chapel Hill.

Turner, Nancy J., and Adam F. Szczawinski. 1991. *Common poisonous plants and mushrooms of North America.* Timber Press, Portland, Oregon.

Van Matre, Steve. 1990. *Earth education...a new beginning.* Institute for Earth Education, Warrenville, IL.

Van Matre, Steve, and Bruce Johnson. 1987. *Earthkeepers.* Institute for Earth Education, Warrenville, IL.

Waldrop, M. Mitchell. 1987. Causality, structure, and common sense. *Science* 237:1297-1299.

Warren, Louis A. 1959. *Lincoln's youth, Indiana years, 1816-1830.* Appleton-Century-Crofts, N.Y.

White, Robin. 1991. Planting seeds in a concrete jungle. Pp. 363-366 in Koopman, Richard W., ed. *Proceedings 1991 National Interpreters Workshop.* NAI, Fort Collins.

Williams, Francis X. 1917. Notes on the life-history of some North American Lampyridae. *J. New York Entomol. Soc.* 25:11-33.

Woods, Thomas A. 1989. Perspectivistic interpretation: a new direction for sites and exhibits. *History News,* January/February 1989:26-28.

Young, Ed. (Publication date not found). *Seven blind mice.* Philomel Books, N.Y.

Zabel, Cynthia, and Spencer Taggart. 1989. Shift in red fox, *Vulpes vulpes,* mating system associated with *El Niño* in the Bering Sea. *Animal Behaviour* 38:830-838.

Zuefle, David Matthew. 1994. *The interface of religious beliefs and environmental values within the interpretive profession: a multimethodological exploratory study.* Ph.D Dissertation, Texas A&M University.

Zweig, Connie, and Jeremiah Abrams, eds. 1991. *Meeting the shadow: the hidden power of the dark side of human nature.* Jeremy P. Tarcher, Inc., Los Angeles.

Index